VIKING
MYTHS & LEGENDS

* * *

The author would like to thank
John Dunne and Kate Brown
for their help in producing this book.

First published in Great Britain by Brockhampton Press, a member of the Hodder Headline Group,
20 Bloomsbury Street, London WC1B 3QA.

Copyright © 1998 Brockhampton Press.

All rights reserved. No part of this publication may be reproduced, stored in a retrieval system, or transmitted, in any form or by any means, without the prior written permission of the copyright holder.

ISBN 1 86019 382 X

A copy of the CIP data is available from the British Library upon request.

Created and produced by Flame Tree Publishing, a part of The Foundry Creative Media Company Limited,
The Long House, Antrobus Road, Chiswick, London W4 5HY.

VIKING
Myths & Legends

K. E. SULLIVAN

CONTENTS

INTRODUCTION

We shall tread once more that well-known plain
Of Ida, and among the grass shall find
The golden dice with which we play'd of yore;
And that will bring to mind the former life
And pastime of the Gods, the wise discourse
Of Odin, the delights of other days.

MATTHEW ARNOLD, *BALDER DEAD*

 HE VIKINGS (VIKINGAR) WERE MEN OF THE NORTH, the inhabitants of Scandinavia who were best known in Europe for their raids throughout the ninth and eleventh centuries. Across history, Vikings have been portrayed as blood-thirsty, passionate and violent savages who looted and plundered England and the coasts of Europe for their own gain. Indeed, the English monk Alcuin wrote, 'Never before has such a terror appeared in Britain as we have now suffered from a pagan race.' The Vikings were a fierce people, and as well as having an intense desire for wealth, power and adventure, they were encouraged by King Harold I to look for foreign conquests. As 'Norsemen' their impact was particularly profound in Northern France, where they began to sail up French rivers, looting and burning the cities of Rouen and Paris, among others, destroying what navigation and commerce they could find. Their ships were spectacular, the finest ever built, and they were able to travel great distances – in the end their quest for adventure and the overpopulation and internal problems in Scandinavia drove them as far as North America and Greenland, where they raided and then settled, showing little regard for existing cultures and religions.

It was these activities which gave the Vikings their reputation, one which has shifted little since the tenth century. Even in 1911, G. K. Chesterton, wrote:

Their souls were drifting as the sea,
And all good towns and lands
They only saw with heavy eyes,
And broke with heavy hands.

Their gods were sadder than the sea
Gods of a wandering will,
Who cried for blood like beasts at night,
Sadly from hill to hill.

Opposite:
The mythology of the Vikings was dramatic and profound; their gods and goddesses were passionate and provocative.

These heavy-handed, great men spoke a strange language and their brutality and lack of regard for Christianity in Europe gave them a reputation as being men of little culture, and certainly men of no religion. Very few Vikings were able to write, and most religious, spiritual and cultural documents were transmitted by word of mouth, or

through their art. Because they carried with them little that explained their origins and their beliefs, and because they did not have an obvious pantheon and system of belief and scripture, it was many years before their new countries developed any real understanding of the Viking religions and mythology.

There was no one religion common to all the Scandinavian and Teutonic peoples, but descriptions from Icelandic texts indicate that most had similar polytheistic features. In early times two groups of gods were worshipped, the Aesir and the Vanir; later they were joined to form a single pantheon of twelve principal deities, headed by Woden (Odin) and including Tiw (Tyr), Thor (Donar), Balder, Frey, Freyia, and Frigga. Their home was Asgard. There, in the palace Valhalla, Odin and his warrior maidens (the Valkyries) gave banquets to dead heroes. Unlike the gods of most religions, the ancient Nordic deities were subject to Fate (represented by the Norns), and tradition held that they were doomed to eventual destruction by the forces of evil in the form of giants and demons, led by Loki. After a savage battle at Ragnarok, the universe would end in a great fire. But from the burning wreckage of the universe would spring a new cosmos, and a new generation of gods and humans would live together harmoniously.

There was a host of rituals, most of which have not survived the passage of time, but magic rites and prayer played an important part in most people's daily lives. Christianity was established quite late in Scandinavia. Denmark moved towards this religion in the tenth century, with Norway converting slightly later and Sweden some one hundred years later than that. The Vikings formally adopted Christianity in about 1000, although their invading parties may have become Christians earlier than that. The advent of Christianity naturally changed the ethos and ritual of the Vikings, but it is important to understand that the Viking mythology was not intrinsic to their religion, as it is in many other cultures, and it was perfectly possible to believe in both Frey, who could encourage fertility in their land, as it was to believe in Christ, who had little to do with their daily lives. It has been said that the Vikings were easily converted to Christianity, for their own gods were not infallible, and could be influenced by fate and events beyond their control. The invincibility of Christ must have seemed very attractive to a people who struggled to put their faith in something or someone that had an ability to overcome the dramatic events that occurred in the North. Some believe that Christian myth may have been incorporated in Norse myth, and because there is little record of early myth, it is difficult to know what the Vikings really believed.

The term mythology means different things in every culture. Broadly speaking mythology is the collective myths of a people and scientific study of these myths, which can be described as traditional stories occurring in a timeless past and involving supernatural elements. In ancient cultures, myths were used to express and explain such serious concerns as the creation of the universe and of humanity, the evolution of society, and the cycle of agricultural fertility. Legends, by contrast with myths, are thought to contain some actual historical elements. Many theories have been advanced to explain myths. Theologians have tended to view myths as foreshadowings or corruptions of Scripture. Sir James Frazer in his *The Golden Bough* (1890) proposed that all myths were originally connected with the idea of fertility in nature, with the birth, death, and resurrection of vegetation as a constantly recurring motif.

Opposite: The English monk Alcuin wrote of the Vikings, 'Never before has such a terror appeared in Britain as we have now suffered from a pagan race.'

But in reality, it is likely that myths were woven around historical fact, real people and events and places that truly existed. In this form they are legends, exaggerated, surely, distorted to make them tellable, more exciting, but created in order to present the moral message of an event which has had some significance in the lives of those touched by it. There were folktales, too, which are tales of enchantment, deceit and trickery, in

which gods and goddesses live alongside talking animals, giants, dwarfs and trolls. Folktales are based on magic, and used to explain phenomenon which may otherwise, to a mind uneducated in science, be frightening and inexplicable. Folktales provide explanations for the wind, the trees, the weather, for echoes, ghosts and seasons. The mythology of the Vikings was never a direct representation of their religion, and the origin of many beliefs was dismissed in the fabric of their legends. Indeed, in *Northern Mythology*, Kauffmann writes, 'His eye was fixed on the mountains till the snowy peaks assumed human features, and the giant of the rock or the ice descended with heavy tread; or he would gaze at the splendour of the spring, or of the summer fields, till Freyia with the gleaming necklace stepped forth, or Sif with the flowing lock of gold'.

There seems to be an almost wry acceptance that their mythology has been created by them, and that the events within it have not occurred and been recorded. H. A. Guerber in *The Norsemen* writes, 'The most distinctive traits of this mythology are a peculiar grim humour, to be found in the religion of no other place, and a dark thread of tragedy which runs throughout the whole woof, and these characteristics, touching both extremes, are writ large over English literature.'

Some of their myths reflected an uncertain religiosity. There are myths of philosophy, addressing matters which concern all of us. They relate to the conception of the world, to death and to living, to gods and to the state of godliness. They may deal with matters relating to a specific tribe, culture or people, making sense of rituals, superstitions and routines. The Vikings lived in a vast, and extreme land, where Nature conspired to quench them in eternal darkness, or burn them with everlasting day; it is not surprising that their mythology took as its central theme the endless struggle of man against Nature. The landscape was at times a frozen, barren wasteland, glittering in the darkness as sharp mountains thrust their way towards a midnight sun, great icy waves crashing icebergs against the violent coastline. And then it was alive, plains and hills bursting with greenery waving in the summer skies that became intense with heat. The contradictions in the climate, in the geography of Scandinavia are reflected in the dramatic mythology of her people. Gwyn Jones, in *The History of the Vikings*, wrote: 'The long, flat, wind-swept wastes of Jultand, the axe-resisting, isolative forests of central Sweden, the sundered Bothnian archipelago, the mountain wildernesses of the Keel, the hostile frozen tundra of the north, and perhaps most of all the fjords, islands, and skerried waterways of the west Norwegian coast – when we add to these distance, cold and the intimidating darkness of winter, when we add, too, the drama of power and delusions of grandeur which built and rebuilt and shattered and reshattered the northern realms from long before the Viking age ... we see that Scandinavia could never be the nursery of weaklings.' As such, the land and the people share a tragic and grand persona; it is easy to understand why the Vikings believed that the earth was the product of fire and ice, and why gods could be fallible, and at the mercy of others. It is even easier to understand why their sense of drama is so refined, and yet its implementation so rugged.

The myths and legends of the Vikings have come down to us from three major sources, although what we have is incomplete, and bare of theology, which must have existed in partnership with their mythological beliefs. Jones writes, ' ... [the religion] accounted for the creation of the world, and charted the doom to come. It provided mysteries as transcendent as Odin hanging nine nights on a windswept tree as a sacrifice to himself, and objects of veneration as crude as the embalmed penis of a horse. Like other religions it rejoiced the devout with hidden truth, and contented mere conformers with its sacral and convivial occasions. There was a god for those who lived by wisdom and statecraft, war and

Opposite: The land-scape was at times a frozen, barren wasteland, glittering in the darkness as sharp mountains thrust their way towards a midnight sun.

plunder, trade and seafaring, or the land's increase. Poet, rune-maker, blacksmith, leech, rye-grower, cattle-breeder, king, brewer, each had a god with whom he felt secure; warlocks, men on skis, barren women, brides, all had a deity to turn to. Best of all the powers, attributes, and functions of the gods overlapped so generously that Odin's man, Thor's man, Frey's man and the like could expect to be looked after in every aspect of life and death.'

The first main source of Viking myths and legends is the *Poetic Edda*, a work in old Icelandic that constitutes the most valuable collection in old Norse literature. Also called the 'Elder' Edda, it is made up of thirty-four mythological and heroic lays, of various lengths. It was written in the second half of the thirteenth century, after the Vikings had accepted Christianity, and therefore the mythology may be influenced by other cultures and beliefs. Although the *Poetic Edda* was written after Christianity, it is not as easy to ascertain when the poems that make it up were actually composed. Some are clearly pre-Viking, and others relate to the period after Scandinavian civilization moved into the Middle Ages. As the name suggests, the works are all poetic, stanzaic in nature, but other than that there is very little linking the various works that comprise it, and many of the poems included in it are obscure. Guerber writes, 'The religious beliefs of the north are not mirrored with any exactitude in the Elder Edda. Indeed, only a travesty of the faith of our ancestors has been preserved in Norse literature. The early poet loved allegory and his imagination rioted among the conceptions of his fertile muse ... We are told nothing as to sacrificial and religious rites, and all else is omitted which does not pride material for artistic treatment ... regarded as a precious relic of the beginning of Northern poetry rather than a representation of the religious beliefs of the Scandinavians, and these literary fragments bear many signs of the transitions stage wherein the confusion of the old and new faiths is easily apparent.'

Many of the poems are narrative, many taking the form of a parable or proverb. There are also works surrounding rite, mysticism and magic, describing chants and spells and healers.

The second great collection of mythological material is the *Prose Edda*, probably written around 1222 by Snorri Sturluson, who was a wealthy farmer in the service of the Norwegian king Hakon Hakonarson. He was also a poet, and a widely educated man, and the *Prose Edda* forms a treatise on the art of Icelandic poetry and a compendium of Viking mythology. There are four main sections to the book, but it is the last, the 'Hattatal' or 'List of Verse Forms' which has provided such a wealth of information on the mythology, for it explains the mythological allusion common in traditional verse, to help poets who wish to recreate it get the facts straight.

R. I. Page, in *Norse Myths*, writes: ' ... Snorri too was a Christian, and could hardly tell such tales as though they were truth, particularly tales that related adventures of the pagan gods. So he distanced himself from the subject in a number of ways. He composed a prologue full of early anthropological observation: how in primitive times men realized there was order in the universe, and deduced it must have a rule; how the most splendid of early communities was Troy in Turkey, with twelve kingdoms each with a prince of superhuman qualities, and one high king above all ...'

Snorri often quotes from the *Poetic Edda*, and in many cases expands ideas and philosophies introduced but never carried to term in the first book. The major failing of the work is the fact that Snorri never manages to place the mythology of the Vikings in any kind of real religious context, by explaining theology or worship. His accounts are very much tainted by his Christianity, and he often takes an orthodox Christian position, identifying the pagan gods and heroes deified by their pagan and therefore ignorant followers.

But the work is lively, witty and full of splendid details; much of the information takes the form of an inventive narrative, in which a chieftain called Odin leads a conquering army into

Sweden, where he is welcomed by a king called Gylfi. Gylfi has a series of questions for the Aesir, as the conquerors were called, and these questions and answers are recounted in the *Prose Edda*, in the form of a fascinating account of lore, folktale and legend.

The third major source for Viking mythology is the work of the court poets or 'skalds'. Skaldic verse comprise a confusion of contemporary events interspersed with works from the Viking ages into the Middle ages and the advent of Christianity. Again, because these works were written after the conversion to Christianity, there have undoubtedly been alterations to the fabric of the myths and it is unlikely that the transmission of the oral tradition has been entirely accurate. But there are many mythological tales which form the subject of the skalds' verse, and there are several notable writers; however, the poetry was normally very elaborate and often technically pretentious, making it difficult to follow in parts.

To this day, little is understood about the myth and religion of the North – partly because it was not successfully transcribed, and partly because their patterns of worship were not directed by conventional piety and are therefore more difficult to understand. Theirs was a traditionally pagan culture, religion and ideology, one in which the seasons, the land, the patterns of daily life were bound up in a simple pantheon of gods and goddesses who were in charge of each aspect of it. Most gods were interrelated, most could help with the never-ending battle against the elements and the brutal geography. In the end their mythology vanished into little more than literature, and as Eric Sharpe wrote, '… the old myths failed because they lacked consistency and seriousness. Odin was treacherous, Christ was not. Thor could be hoodwinked. Christ could not … the old religion had no centre, either in ritual or organizational terms. It was a conglomeration of separate elements and functions, which remain to challenge and sometimes puzzle us. But there is often a certain nostalgia among us … for the memory of men and women who could, for a time at least, shoulder fate aside and worship Thor, because they believed in their own strength.'

How much is genuine Viking legend is difficult to ascertain; what is certain is that the sagas and myths which exist are dramatic, exciting, darkly humorous and passionate. If the role of myth is to entertain, it has undoubtedly succeeded, whatever its source.

We shall see emerge
From the bright Ocean at our feet an earth
More fresh, more verdant than the last, with fruits
Self-springing, and a seed of man preserved,
Who then shall live in peace, as then in war.

MATTHEW ARNOLD, *BALDER DEAD*

✳   ✳   ✳

AUTHOR'S NOTE

The absence of an authoritative source for the myths and legends of the Viking culture means that there are a wide variety of interpretations and series of events which are often not homogeneous. There are fewer principal deities than there are in many other cultures, but the gods and goddesses of Viking mythology are the subjects of often vast sagas and inter-related legends. It is beyond the scope of this book to retell more than a handful of events. You'll find here a selection of evocative and enchanting myths and legends, most well-known, all of which have had a lasting impression on our culture, and each of which characterizes the drama and passion intrinsic to the Viking ideology. The myths and legends which follow are often combinations of several versions, including those of the *Prose Edda*, R. I. Page, H. A. Guerber, and various other more dramatic interpretations. The author acknowledges their essential contribution to what follows.

THE CREATION MYTHS

It was in distant times
When nothing was;
Neither sand nor sea
Nor chill waves;
No earth at all;
Nor the high heavens;
The great void only
And growth nowhere.

MATTHEW ARNOLD, *BALDER DEAD*

HE DRAMATIC CONTRADICTIONS of the Viking landscape and the constant battle with the elements; the spectacular backdrop of perpetual darkness and then perpetual light provide a mythology of profound contrasts. The creation myths are no exception. It was believed that cold was malevolent, evil, and that heat was good and light; when the two meet – when fire meets ice – there comes into existence a cosmos from which the universe can be created. The myths are filled with frost and fire; they are allusive and incomplete; the images and events are impossible and unlinked. But the creation myths of the Viking people are supremely beautiful, and explain, in a way that only a people in a wilderness could conceive, how we came to be.

The Creation of the Universe

Under the armpit grew,
'Tis said of Hrim-thurs,
A girl and boy together;
Foot with foot begat,
Of that wise Jotun,
A six-headed son.

SAEMUND'S EDDA

IN THE BEGINNING, before there was anything at all, there was a nothingness that stretched as far as there was space. There was no sand, nor sea, no waves nor earth nor heavens. And that space was a void that called to be filled, for its emptiness echoed with a deep and frozen silence. So it was that a land sprung up within that silence, and it took the place of half the universe. It was a land called Filheim, or land of fog, and where it ended sprung another land, where the air burned and blazed. This land was called Muspell. Where the regions met lay a great and profound void, called Ginnungagap, and here a peaceful river flowed, softly spreading into the frosty depths of the void where it froze, layer upon layer, until it formed a fundament. And it was here the heat from Muspell licked at the cold of Filheim until the energy they created spawned the great frost-giant Ymir. Ymir was the greatest and the first of all frost-giants, and his part in the creation of the universe led the frost-giants to believe that they should reign supreme on what he had made.

Filheim had existed for many ages, long before our own earth was created. In the centre was a mighty fountain and it was called Vergelmir, and from that great fountain all the rivers of the universe bubbled and stormed. There was another fountain called Elivagar (although some believe that it is the same fountain with a different name), and from this bubbled up a poisonous mass, which hardened into black ice. Elivagar is the beginning of evil, for goodness can never be black.

Muspell burned with eternal light and her heat was guarded by the flame giant, Surtr, who lashed at the air with his great sabre, filling it with glittering sparks of pure heat. Surtr was the fiercest of the fire giants who would one day make Muspell their home. The word Muspell means 'home of the destroyers of the world' and that description is both frightening and accurate because the fire giants were the most terrifying there were.

Opposite:
It was here the heat from Muspell licked at the cold of Filheim until the energy they created spawned the great frost-giant Ymir.

On the other side of the slowly filling chasm, Filheim lay in perpetual darkness, bathed in mists which circled and spun until all was masked. Here, between these stark contrasts, Ymir grew, the personification of the frozen ocean, the product of chaos. Fire and ice met here, and it was these profound contrasts that created a phenomenon like no other, and this was life itself. In the chasm another form was created by the frozen river, where the sparks of the Surtr's sabre caused the ice to drip, and to thaw, and then, when they rested, allowed it to freeze once again. This form was Audhumla, a cow who became known as the nourisher. Her udders were swollen with rich, pure milk, and Ymir drank greedily from the four rivers which formed from them.

Audhumla was a vast creature, spreading across the space where the fire met the ice. Her legs were columns, and they held up the corners of space.

Audhumla, the cow, also needed sustenance, and so she licked at the rime-stones which had formed from the crusted ice, and from these stones she drew salt from the depths of the earth. Audhumla licked continuously, and soon there appeared, under her thirsty tongue, the form of a god. On the first day there appeared hair, and on the second, a head. On the third day the whole god was freed from the ice and he stepped forth as Buri, also called the Producer. Buri was beautiful. He had taken the golden flames of the fire, which gave him a warm, gilded glow, and from the frost and ice he had drawn a purity, a freshness that could never be matched.

While Audhumla licked, Ymir slept, sated by the warmth of her milk. Under his arms the perspiration formed a son and a daughter, and his feet produced a giant called Thrudgemir, an evil frost-giant with six heads who went on to bear his own son, the giant Bergelmir. These were the first of the race of frost-giants.

Buri himself had produced a son, called Borr, which is another word for 'born', and as Buri and Borr became aware of the giants, an eternal battle was begun – one which is to this day waged on all parts of earth and heaven.

For giants represent evil in its many forms, and gods represent all that is good, and on that fateful day the fundamental conflict between them began – a cosmic battle which would create the world as we know it.

Buri and Borr fought against the giants, but by the close of each day a stalemate existed. And so it was that Borr married the giantess Bestla, who was the daughter of Bolthorn, or the thorn of evil. Bestla was to give him three fine, strong sons: Odin, Vili and Ve and with the combined forces of these brave boys, Borr was able to destroy the great Ymir. As they slayed him, a tremendous flood burst forth from his body, covering the earth and all the evil beings who inhabited it with his rich red blood.

The Creation of the Earth

Of Ymir's flesh
Was earth created,
Of his blood the sea,
Of his bones the hills,
Of his hair trees and plants,
Of his skull the heavens,
And of his brows
The gentle powers
Formed Midgard for the sons of men;
But of his brain
The heavy clouds are
All created.

R. B. ANDERSON

YMIR'S BODY WAS CARRIED BY ODIN and his brothers to Ginnungagap, where it was placed in the centre. His flesh became the earth, and his skeleton the rocky crags which dipped and soared. From the soil sprang dwarfs, spontaneously, and they would soon be put to work. Ymir's teeth and shards of broken bones became the rocks and pits covering the earth and his blood was cleared to become the seas and waters that flowed across the land. The three men worked hard on the body of Ymir; his vast size meant that even a day's work would alter the corpse only slightly.

Ymir's skull became the sky and at each cardinal point of the compass was placed a dwarf whose supreme job it was to support it. These dwarfs were Nordri, Sudri, Austri and Westri and it was from these brave and sturdy dwarfs that the terms North, South, East and West were born. Ymir's hair created trees and bushes.

The brow of Ymir became walls which would protect the gods from all evil creatures, and in the very centre of these brows was Midgard, or 'middle garden', where humans could live safely.

Now almost all of the giants had fallen with the death of Ymir,

drowned by his surging blood – all, that is, except Bergelmir, who escaped in a boat with his wife and sought asylum at the edge of the world. Here he created a new world, Jotunheim, or the home of the giants, where he set about the creation of a whole new breed of giants who would carry on his evil deeds.

Odin and his brothers had not yet completed their work. As the earth took on its present form, they slaved at Ymir's corpse to create greater and finer things. Ymir's brains were thrust into the skies to become clouds, and in order to light this new world, they secured the sparks from Surtr's sabre and dotted them among the clouds. The finest sparks were put to one side and they studded the heavenly vault with them; they became like glittering stars in the darkness. The stars were given positions; some were told to pass forward, and then back again in the heavens. This provided seasons, which were duly recorded.

The brightest of the remaining stars were joined together to become the sun and the moon, and they were sent out into the darkness in gleaming gold chariots. The chariots were drawn by Arvakr (the early waker) and Alsvin (the rapid goer), two magnificent white horses under whom were placed balls of cool air which had been trapped in great skins. A shield was placed before the sun so that her rays would not harm the milky hides of the steeds as they travelled into the darkness.

Although the moon and the sun had now been created, and they were sent out on their chariots, there was still no distinction between day and night, and that is a story of its own.

Night and Day

Forth from the east, up the ascent of heaven.
Day drove his courser with the shining mane.

MATTHEW ARNOLD, *BALDER DEAD*

THE CHARIOTS WERE READY, and the steeds were bursting at their harnesses to tend to the prestigious task of setting night and day in place. But who would guide them? The horses would need leadership of some sort, and so it was decided that the beautiful children of the giant Mundilfari – Mani (the moon) and Sol (the sun) would be given the direction of the steeds. And at once, they were launched into the heavens.

Opposite: Ymir's brains were thrust into the skies to become clouds, and the world was now near to being complete; the god's own palaces would soon be built.

Next, Nott (night), who was daughter of one of the giants, Norvi, was provided with a rich black chariot which was drawn by a lustrous stallion called Hrim-faxi (frost mane). From his mane, the frost and dew were sent down to the earth in glimmering baubles. Nott was a goddess, and she had produced three children, each with a different father. From Naglfari, she had a son named Aud; Annar, her second husband, gave her Jord (earth), and with her third husband, the god Dellinger, a son was born and he was called Dag (day).

Dag was the most radiant of her children, and his beauty caused all who saw him to bend down in tears of rapture. He was given his own great chariot, drawn by a perfect white horse called Skin-faxi (shining mane), and as they travelled, wondrous beams of light shot out in every direction, brightening every dark corner of the world and providing much happiness to all.

Many believe that the chariots flew so quickly, and continued their journey round and round the world because they were pursued by wolves: Skoll (repulsion) and Hati (hatred). These evil wolves sought a way to create eternal darkness and like the perpetual battle of good and evil, there could be no end to their chase.

Mani brought along in his chariot Hiuki, who represented the waxing moon, and Bil, who was the waning moon. And so it was that Sun, Moon, Day and Night were in place, with Evening, Midnight, Morning, Forenoon, Noon and Afternoon sent to accompany them. Summer and Winter were rulers of all seasons: Summer was a popular and warm god, a descendant of Svasud. Winter, was an enemy for he represented all that contrasted with Summer, including the icy winds which blew cold and unhappiness over the earth. It was believed that the great frost-giant Hraesvelgr sat on the extreme north of the heavens and that he sent the frozen winds across the land, blighting all with their blasts of icy death.

The First Humans

There in the Temple, carved in wood,
The image of great Odin stood.

HENRY WADSWORTH LONGFELLOW,
SAGA OF KING OLAF

ODIN, ALLFATHER, WAS KING OF ALL GODS, and he travelled across the newly created earth with his brothers Vili and Ve. Vili was now known as Hoenir, and Ve had become Lothur, or Loki. One morning, the three brothers walked together on the shores of the ocean, looking around with pride at the new world around them. Ymir's body had been well distributed, and his blood now ran clear and pure as the ocean, with the fresh new air sparkling above it all. The winds blew padded clouds across a perfect blue sky, and there was happiness all around. But, and there was no mistaking it, there was silence.

The brothers looked at one another, and then looked out across the crisp sands. There lay on the shore two pieces of driftwood which had been flung onto the coast from the sea, and as their eyes caught sight of them, each brother shared the same thought. They raced towards the wood, and Hoenir stood over the first piece, so that his shadow lay across it and the wood appeared at once to have arms and legs. Loki did the same with the second piece of wood, but he moved rather more animatedly, so that the wood appeared to dance in the sunlight. And then Odin bent down and blew a great divine breath across the first piece of wood. There in front of them, the bark, the water-soaked edges of the log began to peel away, and there the body of a pale, naked woman appeared. She

Opposite:
The winds blew padded clouds across a perfect sky, and there was happiness all around. But, and there was no mistaking it, there was silence.

lay there, still and not breathing. Odin moved over to the next piece of wood, and he blew once more. Again, the wood curled back to reveal the body of a naked man. He lay as still as the woman.

Odin had given the gift of life to the man and woman, and they had become entities with a soul and a mind. It was now time for Loki to offer his own gifts. He stood at once over the woman and as he bent over her, he transferred the blush of youth, the power of comprehension, and the five senses of touch, smell, sight, hearing and taste. He was rewarded when the woman rose then and smiled unquestioningly at the three gods. She looked around in wonder, and then down at the lifeless body by her side. And Loki leaned across the body of man this time, and gave to him blood, which began to run through his veins. He too received the gifts of understanding, and of the five senses, and he was able to join woman as she stood on the beach.

Hoenir stepped forward then, and offered to both man and woman the power of speech. At this, the two human beings turned and walked together into the new world, their hands held tightly together.

'Stop,' said Odin, with great authority.

Turning, the two humans looked at him and nodded. 'You are Ash,' said Odin to the man, which represented the tree from which he had been created. 'And you are Elm,' he said to the woman. Then Odin leaned over and draped his cloak around the shoulders of the first human woman and sent her on her way, safe in the care of man, who would continue in that role until the end of time – or so the Vikings said.

Asgard

From the hall of Heaven he rose away
To Lidskialf, and sate upon his throne,
The mount, from whence his eye surveys the world.
And far from Heaven he turned his shining orbs
To look on Midgard, and the earth, and men.

MATTHEW ARNOLD, *BALDER DEAD*

Opposite:
Odin, Hoenir and Loki walked together on the shores of the ocean, looking around with pride at their creation.

ASGARD IS ANOTHER WORD for 'enclosure of the gods'. It was a place of great peace, ruled by Odin and built by Odin and his sons on Yggdrasill, above the clouds, and centred over Midgard. Each of the palaces of Asgard was built for pleasure, and only things which were

perfect in every way could become part of this wondrous land. The first palace built was Gladsheim, or Joyous home, and it was created to house the twelve thrones of the principal deities. Everything was cast from gold, and it shone in the heavens like the sun itself. A second palace was built for the goddesses, and it was called Vingof, or Friendly Floor. Here, too, everything was made from gold, which is the reason why Asgard's heyday became known as the golden years.

As Asgard was conceived, and built, a council was held, and the rules were set down for gods and goddesses alike. It was decreed at this time that there would be no blood shed within the limits of the realm, and that harmony would reign forever. A forge was built, and all of the weapons and tools required for the construction of the magnificent palaces were made there. The gods held their council at the foot of Yggdrasill, and in order to travel there, a bridge was erected – the rainbow bridge, or Bifrost as it became known. The bridge arched over Midgard, on either side of Filheim, and its colours were so spectacular that one could only gaze in awe upon seeing them for the first time.

The centre of Asgard displayed the plan of Idavale, with hills that dipped and soared with life. Here the great palaces were set in lush green grasses. One was Breibalik, or Broad Gleaming, and there was Glitnir, in which all was made gold and silver. There were palaces clustered in gems, polished and shimmering in the light of the new heavens. And that beauty of Asgard was reflected by the beauteous inhabitants – whose minds and spirits were pure and true. Asgard was the home of all the Aesir, and the setting for most of the legends told here. But there was another family of

gods – and they were called the Vanir.

For many years the Vanir lived in their own land, Vanaheim, but the time came when a dispute arose between the two families of gods, and the Aesir waged war against the Vanir. In time, they learned that unity was the only way to move forward, and they put aside their differences and drew strength from their combined forces. In order to ratify their treaty, each side took hostages. So it was that Niord came to dwell in Asgard with Frey and Freyia, and Hoenir went to live in Vanaheim, the ultimate sacrifice by one of the brothers of creation.

Yggdrasill

*I know that I hung
On a wind-rocked tree
Nine whole nights,
With a spear wounded,
And to Odin offered
Myself to myself;
On that tree
Of which no one knows
From what root it springs.*

ODIN'S RUNE SONG

YGGDRASILL IS THE WORLD ASH, a tree that has been there for all time, and will always be there. Its branches overhang all nine worlds, and they are linked by the great tree. The roots of the Yggdrasill are tended by the Norns, three powerful sisters who are also called the fates. The roots are nourished by three wells. One root reaches into Asgard, the domain of the gods, and feeds from the well of Wyrd, which is the name of the eldest Norn. The second root leads to Jotunheim, the land of the frost-giants. The well at the end of this root is called Mimir, who was once a god. Only the head of Mimir has survived the creation of the world, and it drinks daily from the well and is kept alive by the magic herbs which are scattered in it. Mimir represents great wisdom, and even Odin chose to visit him there to find answers to the most profound questions that troubled his people.

The third root winds its way to Filheim, and the well here is the scum-filled fountain of black water called Vergelmir. Here, the

Opposite: Here the palaces were set in lush green grasses, on the banks of gurgling rivers, wreathed by rich, white clouds and mists which swirled across their glittering surfaces.

root of the tree is poisoned, gnawed upon, and from it rises the scent of death and dying. In Vergelmir is a great winged dragon called Nithog, and he sits at the base of the root and inflicts damage that would have caused another tree to wither away.

And the magnificent tree stands, as it has always stood, as the foundation of each world, and a point of communication between all. The name Yggdrasill has many evil connotations, and translated it means 'Steed of Ygg' or, 'Steed of Odin'. There once was a time when Odin longed to know the secret of runes – the symbols which became writing, as we know it. The understanding of runes was a cherished one, and in order to acquire it, a terrible sacrifice must be undergone by the learner. Odin had longed for many years to have that knowledge, and the day came when he was prepared to make his sacrifice. Odin was told that he must hang himself by the neck from the bough of the World Ash, and he must remain there, swinging in the frozen anarchy of the dark winds, for nine days. The story has been told that Odin, the bravest of the gods, the father of all, screamed with such terror and pain that the gods held their hands to their ears for each of those nine wretched days.

But Odin's strength of character carried him through the tortuous ordeal and so it was that he was at once the master of the magic runes, the only bearer of the secret along the length of the great tree. His knowledge was shared amongst his friends and his wisdom became legendary.

Odin was at the helm of the nine worlds, which stretched from Asgard in the topmost branches, to the world of Hel down below, at the lowest root. In between were the worlds of the Vanir, called Vanaheim,

Opposite:
Odin faced a terrible sacrifice in order to learn the secrets of the runes, but his strength of character carried him through the tortuous ordeal.

Midgard, where humans lived, as well as the worlds of the light elves, the dark elves, the dwarfs, the frost and hill giants and, at last, the fire-giants of Muspell. The most magnificent, and the world we hear the most about was Asgard, and it is here that our story begins.

❋ ❋ ❋

LEGENDS OF ODIN AND ASGARD

Sokvabek Hight the fourth dwelling;
Over it flow the cool billows;
Glad drink there Odin and Saga
Every day from golden cups.

R. B. ANDERSON, *NORSE MYTHOLOGY*

n the golden age of Asgard, Odin reigned at the head of the nine worlds of Yggdrasill. He was a fair man, well-liked by all, and his kingdom of Asgard was a magnificent place, where time stood still and youth and the pleasures of nature abounded. Odin was also called Allfather, for he was the father of all men and gods. He reigned high on his throne, overlooking each of the worlds, and when the impulse struck him, Odin disguised himself and went among the gods and people of the other worlds, seeking to understand their activities. Odin appeared in many forms, but he was often recognized for he had just one eye, and that eye could see all. Odin had many adventures, and before the war of the gods, before Odin began to prepare for Ragnarok, Asgard was a setting for many of them, as you will see. All of the gods have their stories, and some of the most exciting are recorded here.

Odin and Frigga in Asgard

Easily to be known is,
By those who to Odin come,
The mansion by its aspect.
Its roof with spears is laid,
Its hall with shields is decked,
With corselets are its benches strewed.

LAY OF GRIMNIR

ODIN WAS THE SON OF BOR, and the brother of Vili and Ve. He was the most supreme god of the Northern races and he brought great wisdom to his place at the helm of all gods. He was called Allfather, for all gods were said to have descended from him, and his esteemed seat was Asgard itself. He held a throne there, one in an exalted and prestigious position, and it served as a fine watchtower from which he could look over men on earth, and the other gods in Asgard as they went about their daily business.

Odin was a tall, mighty warrior. While not having the brawn of many excellent men, he had wisdom which counted for much more. On his shoulders he carried two ravens, Hugin (thought) and Munin (Memory), and they perched there, as he sat on his throne, and recounted to him the activities in the great wide world. Hugin and Munin were Odin's eyes and his ears when he was in Asgard and he depended on their bright eyes and alert ears for news of everything that transpired down below. In his hand Odin carried a great spear, Gungnir, which had been forged by dwarfs, and which was so sacred that it could never be broken. On his finger Odin wore a ring, Draupnir, which represented fertility and fruitfulness and which was more valuable to him, and to his land, than anything in any other god's possession. At the foot of Odin's throne sat two wolves or hunting hounds, Geri and Freki, and these animals were sacred. If one happened upon them while hunting, success was assured.

Odin belonged to a mysterious region, somewhere between life and death. He was more subtle and more dangerous than any of the other gods, and his name in some dialects means 'wind', for he could be both forceful and gentle, and then elusive or absent. On the battlefield, Odin would dress as an old man – indeed, Odin had many disguises, for when things changed in Asgard, and became bad, he had reason to travel on the earth to uncover many secrets – attended by ravens, wolves and the Valkyries, who were the 'choosers of the slain', the maidens who took the souls of fallen warriors to Valhalla.

Valhalla was Odin's palace at Asgard, and its grandeur was breathtaking. Valhalla means 'hall of the chosen slain', and it had five hundred great wooden doors, which were wide enough to allow eight hundred warriors to pass, breastplate to breastplate. The walls were made of glittering spears, polished until they gleamed like silver, and the roof was a sea of golden shields which shone like the sun itself. In Odin's great hall were huge banqueting tables, where the Einheriar, or warriors favoured by Odin, were served. The tables were laden with the finest horns of mead, and platters of roast boar. Like everything else in Asgard, Valhalla was enchanted. Even the boar was divine and Saehrimnir, as he was called, was slain daily by the cook, boiled and roasted and served each night in tender, succulent morsels, and then brought back to life again the following day, for the procedure to take place once again. After the meal, the warriors would retire to the palace forecourt where they would engage in unmatched feats of arms for all to see. Those who were injured would be healed instantly by the enchantment of Valhalla, and those who watched became even finer warriors.

Odin lived in Asgard with Frigga, who was the mother-goddess and his wife. Frigga was daughter of Fiogyn and sister of Jord, and she was greatly beloved on earth and in Asgard. She was goddess of the atmosphere and the clouds, and she wore garments that were as white as the snow-laden mountains that gently touched the land of Asgard. As mother of all, Frigga carried about her a heady scent of the earth – blossoming flowers, ripened fruit, and luscious greenery. There are many stories told about Frigga, as we will discover below.

Life in Asgard was one of profound comfort and grace. Each day dawned new and fresh for the passage of time had not been accorded to Asgard and nothing changed except to be renewed. The sun rose each day, never too hot, and the clouds gently cooled the air as the day waned. Each night the sky was lit with glistening stars, and the fresh, rich white moon rose in the sky and lit all with her milky light. There was no evil in Asgard and the good was as pure as the water, as the air, and as the thoughts of each god and goddess as he and she slept.

In the fields, cows grazed on verdant green grass and in the trees birds caught a melody and tossed it from branch to branch until the whole world sang with their splendid music. The wind wove its way through the trees, across the mountains, and under the sea-blue skies – kissing ripples into the streams and turning a leaf to best advantage. There was a peace and harmony that exists for that magical moment just before spring turns to summer, and it was that moment at which Asgard was suspended for all time.

And so it was that Odin and Frigga brought up their young family here, away from the darkness on the other side, far from the clutches of change and disharmony. There were nine worlds in Yggdrasill, the World Ash, which stretched out from Asgard as far as the eye could see. At the top there was Aesir, and in the bottom was the dead world of Hel, at the Tree's lowest roots. In between were the Vanir, the light elves, the dark elves, men, frost and hill giants, dwarfs and the giants of Muspell.

Frigga kept her own palace in Asgard, called Fensalir, and from his high throne Odin could see her there, hard at her work. Frigga's palace was called the hall of mists, and she sat with her spinning wheel, spinning golden thread or long webs of bright-coloured clouds with a marvellous, jewelled spinning wheel which could be seen as a constellation in the night's sky.

There was a story told once of Frigga, one in which her customary goodness and grace were compromised. Frigga was a slim and elegant goddess, and she took great pride in her appearance – something the later Christians would consider to be a sin, but which the Vikings understood, and indeed encouraged. She had long silky hair and she dressed herself in exquisite finery, and Odin showered her with gifts of gems and finely wrought precious metals. She lived contentedly, for her husband was generous, until the day came when she spied a splendid golden ornament which had been fastened to a statue of her husband. As the seamless darkness of Asgard fell one evening, she slipped out and snatched the ornament, entrusting it to dwarfs whom she asked to forge her the finest of necklaces. When the jewel was complete, it was the most beautiful decoration ever seen on any woman – goddess or humankind – and it made her more attractive to Odin so that he plied her with even more gifts, and more love than ever. Soon, however, he discovered that his decoration had been stolen, and he called together all of the dwarfs and with all the fury of a god demanded that this treacherous act be explained. Now Frigga was beloved both by god and dwarf, and although the dwarfs were at risk of death at the hand of Odin, they remained loyal to Frigga, and would not tell Allfather who had stolen the golden ornament.

Odin's anger knew no bounds. The silence of the dwarfs meant only one thing to him – treason – and he swore to find out the real thief by daybreak. And so it was that on that night Odin

Opposite:
The Bifrost, or Rainbow bridge, stretched across Asgard from Midgard; in the distance Frigga's palace, the hall of mists, could be seen.

commanded that the statue be placed above the gates of the palace, and he began to devise runes which would enable it to talk, and to betray the thief. Frigga's blood turned cold when she heard this commandment, for Odin was a kind and generous god when he was happy and content, but when he was crossed, there was a blackness in his nature that put them all in danger. There was every possibility that Frigga would be cast out of Asgard if he were to know of her deceit, and it was at the expense of everything that she intended to keep it a secret.

Frigga called out to her favourite attendant, Fulla, and begged her to find some way to protect her from Odin. Fulla disappeared and several hours later returned with a dwarf, a hideous and frightening dwarf who insisted that he could prevent the secret from being uncovered, if Frigga would do him the honour of smiling kindly on him. Frigga agreed at once, and that night, instead of revealing all, the statue was smashed to pieces while the unwitting guards slept, drugged by the ugly dwarf.

Odin was so enraged by this new travesty that he left Asgard at once – disappearing into the night and taking with him all of the blessings he had laid upon Asgard. And in his absence, Asgard and the worlds around turned cold. Odin's brothers, it is said, stepped into his place, taking on his appearance in order to persuade the gods and men that all was well, but they had not his power or his great goodness and soon enough the frost-giants invaded the earth and cast across the land a white blanket of snow. The trees were stripped of their finery, the sun-kissed streams froze and forgot how to gurgle their happy song. Birds left the trees and cows huddled together in frosty paddocks. The clouds joined together and became an impenetrable mist and the wind howled and scowled through the barren rock.

For seven months Asgard stood frozen until the hearts of each man within it became frosted with unhappiness, and then Odin returned. When he saw the nature of the evil that had stood in his place, he placed the warmth of his blessings on the land once more, forcing the frost-giants to release them. He had missed Frigga, and he showered her once more with love and gifts, and as mother of all gods, once again she took her place beside him as his queen.

Opposite:
Frigga begged Odin not to leave Asgard, for she knew what would happen in the absence of his blessings.

Asgard had many happy days before Frigga's necklace caused the earth to become cold. Frigga and Odin had many children, including Thor, their eldest son, who was the favourite of the gods and the people – a large and boisterous god with a zeal for life. He did everything with great passion, and spirit, and his red hair and red

beard made him instantly identifiable, wherever he went. Thor lived in Asgard at Thruthvangar, in his castle hall Bilskirnir (lightning). He was often seen with a sheet of lightning, which he flashed across the land, ripening the harvest and ensuring good crops for all. With his forked lightning in another hand, he travelled to the edges of the kingdoms, fighting trolls and battling giants, the great guardian of Asgard and of men and gods.

Thruthvangar had five hundred and forty rooms, and it was the largest castle ever created. Here he lived with the beautiful Sif, an exquisite goddess with hair made of long, shining strands of gold. Sif was the goddess of the fields, and the mother of the earth, like Frigga. Her long, golden hair was said to represent the golden grass covering the harvest fields, and Thor was very proud of her.

Balder was the second son of Odin and Frigga at Asgar, and he was the fairest of all the gods – indeed, his purity and goodness shone like a moonbeam and he was so pale as to be translucent. Balder was beloved by all, and his innate kindness caused him to love everything around him – evil or good. He lived in Breidablik, with his wife Nanna.

The third son of Odin was Hodur, a blind but happy god who sat quietly, listening and enjoying the sensual experiences of the wind in his hair, the sun on his shoulders, the joyful cries of the birds on the air. While all was good in Asgar, Hodur was content, and although he represented darkness, and was the twin to Balder's light, that darkness had no real place and it was kept in check by the forces of goodness.

Odin's fourth son was Tyr, who was the most courageous and brave of the gods – the god of martial honour and one of the twelve gods of Asgard. He did not have his own palace, for he travelled widely, but he held a throne at Valhalla, and in the great council hall of Gladsheim. Tyr was also the god of the sword, and every sword had his rune carved into its handle. Although Odin was his father, Tyr's mother is said to have been a beautiful unknown giantess.

Heimdall also lived in Asgard, and he was called the white god, although he was not thought to be the son of Odin and Frigga at all. Some said he had been conceived by nine mysterious sisters, who had given birth to him together. His stronghold was a fort on the boundary of Asgard, next to the Bifrost bridge, and he slept there with one eye open, and both ears alert, for the sound of any enemy approaching.

There were many other gods in Asgard, and many who would one day come to live there. But in those early days of creation, the golden years of Asgard, life was simple, and its occupants few and wondrous. The gods and goddesses lived together in their palaces, many of them with children, about whom many stories can be told.

But even the golden years of Asgard held their secrets, and even the best of worlds must have its serpent. There was one inhabitant of Asgard who no one cared to discuss, the very spirit of evil. He was Loki, who some said was the brother of Odin, although there were others who swore he could not be related to Allfather. Loki was the very personification of trickery, and deceit, and his mischief led him into great trouble. But that is another story.

Heimdall in Midgard

To battle the gods are called
By the ancient
Gjaller-horn.
Loud blows Heimdall,
His sound is in the air.
SAEMUND'S EDDA

HEIMDALL WAS CALLED THE WATCHMAN OF THE GODS, and he was distinguished by his role at the Bifrost bridge, which he had constructed from fire, air and water which glowed as a rainbow in the sky. The Bifrost bridge was also called the Rainbow bridge, and it connected heaven with earth, ending just under the great tree Yggdrasill.

The golden age of Asgard was one of such happiness that there was never any threat to the peace of the land, and so it was that its watchman became bored. Heimdall was easily spotted, so he could not travel far without being recognized and commended for his fine work. He carried over his shoulder a great bugle, Giallarhorn, the blasts of which could summon help from all nine worlds. One fine day, Odin noticed that Heimdall had been hard at work without any respite for many many years. Odin himself would occasionally slip into a disguise in order to go out into the worlds beneath them, and he decided then that Heimdall should have the same opportunity – after all, Asgard was hardly in need of defence when all was quiet.

Heimdall was delighted, for he had been longing to visit Midgard and to get to know the people there. He carefully laid his bugle and his sword to one side, and dressed in the garb of the people of Midgard, he slipped

across the bridge and reached a deserted shore. The first people he clapped
eyes upon were Edda and Ai, a poor couple who lived on the bare beaches of
Midgard, eking a meagre living from the sands. They lived in a tumble-down
shack and had little in their possession, but what they did have they offered
gladly to Heimdall. Their shack was sparsely furnished, with only a seaweed
bed on which to lay, but it was agreed that Heimdall could sleep there with
them, and at night he laid himself between the couple and slept well.

After three nights, Heimdall summoned Ai and Edda as they
gathered snails and cockles from the seashore. He had put together several
pieces of driftwood, and as they watched, he fashioned a pointed stick from
one, and cut out a hole in another. The pointed stick was placed inside the
hole, and he turned it quickly, so that sparks, and then a slender stream of
smoke was produced. And then there was fire. Ai and Edda flew back
against the walls of the shack, astonished by this magical feat. It was then
that Heimdall took his leave from them.

Ai and Edda's lives were transformed by fire. Their water was
heated; the most inedible nuggets from the beach were softened into tender
morsels of food. And most of all, they had warmth. Nine months later a
second gift appeared to Edda, for she gave birth to a son who she called
Thrall. Thrall was an ugly, wretched-looking boy, with a knotted body and a
twisted back, but he was kind and he worked hard. When he came of age,
he married one like him – a deformed young woman called Serf. Together
they had many children, all of whom worked about the house or on the land
with the same diligence as their father and mother. These were the ancestors
of the thralls.

Heimdall had left the home of Ai and Edda and travelled on. Soon
enough he came to a lovely little house occupied by an older couple Amma
and Afi. As he arrived, Afi was hard at work, whittling away at beams with
which to improve their house. Heimdall set down his belongings and began
to work with Afi. Soon they had built together a wonderful loom, which they
presented to Amma, who was seated happily by the fire with her spinning
wheel. Heimdall ate well that evening, and when the time came for sleep, he
was offered a place between them in the only bed. For three nights Heimdall

Opposite: Heimdall was distinguished by his role at the Bifrost bridge, which he had constructed from fire, air and water, and which glowed as a rainbow in the sky.

stayed with Afi and Amma, and then he left them. Sure enough, nine
months later, and to the astonishment of the elderly couple, Amma
gave birth to a son, who they called Karl the Yeoman. Karl was a
thick-set, beautiful boy, with sparkling eyes and cheeks of roses. He
loved the land and the fresh air was almost food enough for him, he

drew so much goodness from it. When he became of age, he married a whirlwind of a woman who saw to it that their household ran as smoothly as a well-oiled rig, and that their children, their oxen and all the other animals on their farm, were fed and comfortable. They grew very successful, and they are the first of the ancestors of the yeoman farmer.

The third visit in Midgard was to a wealthy couple who lived in a fine castle. The man of the household spent many hours honing his hunting bow and spears, and his wife sat prettily by his side, well-dressed and flushed by the heat of the fire in the hearth. They offered him rich and delicious food, and at night he was given a place between them in their luxurious and comfortable bed. Heimdall stayed there for three nights, although he would happily have stayed there forever, after which time he returned to his post at the Bifrost bridge. And so it was, nine months later, that a son was born to that couple in the castle, and they called him Jarl the Earl. His father taught him well the skills of hunting and living off the land, and his mother passed on her refinement and breeding, so that Jarl became known as 'Regal'. When Regal was but a boy, Heimdall returned again to Midgard, and claimed him as his son. Regal remained in Midgard, but his fine pedigree was soon known about the land and he grew to become a great ruler there. He married Erna, who bore him many sons, one of whom was the ancestor of a line of Kings who would rule the land forever.

Heimdall took up his place once more in Asgard, but he was prone to wandering, as all gods are, and there are many more stories of his travels.

Loki

Odin! dost thou remember
When we in early days
Blended our blood together?
When to taste beer
Thou did'st constantly refuse
Unless to both 'twas offered?

SAEMUND'S EDDA

Opposite: Loki was a trickster, whose eyes burned with mischief of the most dangerous kind. His handsome exterior housed a soul that was black and rotten.

LOKI WAS A TRICKSTER, a good-looking rascal of a man whose eyes burned with mischief of the most dangerous kind. His handsome exterior housed a soul that was black and rotten, but for many years he lived happily in Asgard, amusing the gods and causing no real

trouble other than that of a clown, or a fool, and so he was tolerated there, and allowed to marry and have children.

Loki was married to Sigyn, and his children were more terrible than him. He had already three children by an ogress called Angurboda – one a wolf called Fenris, another a serpent or dragon, Jormungander, who overtook Midgard as he grew, and the third, a dark but beautiful child called Hel. She was to become the queen of the underworld, and she had control over every man and woman who entered her gates.

Now Loki's trickery was well known in Asgard, and across the nine worlds, and his story is inextricably linked with that of the other gods, for he involved himself in most events in their lives, offering advice, and annoying them. Some of his mischief was amusing; some was dangerous.

One evening, when Freyia had become part of Asgard, Loki spied her marvellous necklace, a golden symbol of the fruitfulness of the earth which she wore about her slender neck at all times. Loki coveted this necklace, and he found he could not sleep until he had it in his possession. So it was that he crept one night into her chamber and bent over as if to remove it. Finding that her position in sleep made this feat impossible, he turned himself into a small flea, and springing under the bedclothes, he bit the lovely goddess so that she turned in her sleep. Loki returned to his shape and undid the clasp of the necklace, which he removed without rousing Freyia.

Not far from Freyia's palace, Heimdall had heard the sound of Loki becoming a flea – a sound so slight that only the great watchman of the gods could have heard it – and he travelled immediately to the palace to investigate. He saw Loki leaving with the necklace, and soon caught up with him, drawing his sword in order to remove the thief's head. Loki immediately changed himself into a thin blue flame, but quick as a flash, Heimdall became a cloud and sent down a sheath of rain in order to douse the flame. Loki quickly became a polar bear and opened his jaws to swallow the water, whereupon Heimdall turned himself into bear and attacked the hapless trickster. In haste, Loki became a seal, and then, once again, Heimdall transformed himself in the same form as Loki and the two fought for many hours, before Heimdall showed his worth and won the necklace from Loki.

There is another story told of Loki, whose tricks were not always used to ill-effect.

One day, a giant and a peasant sat together playing a game. There were bets laid on the outcome of the game, and the giant won. The peasant, having little to offer, had pledged his only son, and the giant promised to return the following day to claim his prize. The peasant returned to his wife and admitted his shameful problem, and together they prayed to Odin, who answered their prayers and came down to earth. He changed the peasant's boy into a tiny grain of wheat and hid it in a sheaf of grain in the centre of a large wheatfield. But Skrymsli, the giant, was wiser than Allfather had given him credit for, and when he discovered the boy missing from the peasant's home, he walked straight to the wheatfield, located the shaft of wheat and plucked out the grain which was the boy. He was just about to eat it when Odin heard the child's cry and returned to earth once again. He snatched the grain from the hand of Skrymsli, and transformed the boy to his human form once again. He apologized to the peasants and left them, saying that there was no more he could do for them.

Skrymsli roared and shouted that he had been deceived and he vowed that he would return the following day to claim his prize. Once again the peasants prayed, this time to Hoenir, who graciously came to earth and changed the boy into a soft piece of down, which he hid in the breast of a swan who glided easily across the stream by the peasant's home. It was not long before Skrymsli returned, and he took only a few moments to guess what had happened to the boy. Grasping the swan by the neck, he made as if to bite off its head when Hoenir heard the boy's cries and returned to earth. He returned the boy to his parents, but then he disappeared, explaining that he had done all he could to help and could do no more.

The peasants were in great despair, and the giant promised that he would return the following day to claim his prize. They prayed then to Loki, who came down to them at once, carrying the boy out to sea and hiding him in an egg in the roe of a flounder. The giant spied Loki returning from his task, and he guessed at once where the peasant's boy was being held. He captured a boat, and went at once to sea with his fishing rod in hand, and soon enough he captured the flounder. The fish was opened and the egg extracted, when suddenly, Loki reappeared and plucked the egg from the giant's hand, transforming it once again into the boy, who was sent running home to his parents.

Loki set upon the giant then, cutting off his leg and beating him about the head. But Skrymsli had powers of his own, and he was able to heal himself at once, regaining his form and making for the home of the peasants. He was on the brink of capturing the boy when Loki used a clever ploy. He quickly chopped off the leg of the giant, and threw it away so that

it could not be rejoined. He placed a spear of metal where the leg had been, for it was well known that even magic could not cross a metal barrier. The giant was slain at last, and the peasants rejoiced, praising Loki so that he became inflated with pride.

Loki appears many more times in the stories of Asgard, and his name was often on the tongues of its inhabitants.

The Norns

Thence come the maids
Who much do know;
Three from the hall
Beneath the tree;
One they named Was,
And Being next,
The third Shall be.

THE VOLUSPA

THE NORNS ARE SPOKEN OF WITH GREAT RESPECT, for they are the sisters who make their home at the base of Yggdrasill and it is they who protect her great roots. Their home is a cave, and in its centre lies a pool as clear as the air in Asgard. Each day, the Norns take water from that pool and mix it with the enchanted clay and gravel on its banks. This they spread across the roots of Yggdrasill, and then they seat themselves in their cave and begin to spin.

It is the spinning of the Norns which most concerns the inhabitants of Asgard, for the Norns spin time on their spindles and it was from this work that they take their names. The oldest sister is Wyrd, or 'Was', the second sister is Verdandi, or 'Being', and the youngest sister is Skuld, or 'Shall be'. The Norns were also called 'The Fates', and they took up their place at the roots of the tree when evil began to enter Asgard.

Once time had reached Asgard, there was nothing to prevent things from ageing, and it was only with the enchanted apples of Idunn that the gods were able to renew their youth each day. The gods knew they were at the mercy of the Norns and for that reason they chose to consult them daily. Even Odin attended their cave on a regular basis to ask for their advice and aid. The Norns spoke little, and many believed that they could not speak the future, that they spun and spun the web of time at the wish of Orlog, the eternal law of the universe, who had bade them weave at

Opposite: The Norns were often approached by Odin, who attended their cave to ask for advice and aid. They spoke little and many believed they could see the future.

his discretion. But Odin was often advised about the fate of his people – although his own future was kept secret from him and from his fellow gods.

The sisters worked quietly, murmuring a chant as they worked, and the two older sisters in particular were considered beneficent. Wyrd and Verdandi worked without purpose, while the youngest sister, Skuld, was much more purposeful, often destroying the hard work of her sisters for no reason at all.

It was the sisters who predicted the great war in heaven, when the Vanir and the Aesir would begin a civil war that would bring down the walls of Asgard – and allow sin to enter.

Idunn and the Apples

Bright Iduna, Maid immortal!
Standing at Valhalla's portal,
In her casket has rich store
Of rare apples gilded o'er;
Those rare apples, not of Earth,
Ageing Aesir give fresh birth.

J. C. JONES, *VALHALLA*

ONE FINE DAY, ODIN, Loki and Hoenir wandered throughout the worlds on one of their regular missions to see that all was well. As they travelled, they grew hungry, and finally stopped in order to cook an ox to give them sustenance to carry on. A fine ox was chosen from a herd in a field, and it was duly slain and placed on a spit over roaring flames. After several hours, the ox was removed from the fire, and the three wanderers licked their lips and they prepared for their meal. Hoenir cut into the beef, and stopped. Under the crisp exterior, the beef was raw through and through. Fresh blood dripped on to the fire. Hoenir looked puzzled, but he placed the beef back on the spit and motioned to his friends that they could not eat just yet.

The fire was built up once more and the three men waited for another hour or so before removing the beef from the spit once more. This time Odin cut into the meat, but again it was uncooked – it appeared that the fire had had no effect whatsoever.

Suddenly there was a movement in the trees, and a rush of wings. There, at the top of the tree overlooking their fire sat a great eagle. He sat looking down at them with great satisfaction.

Opposite: It was the sisters who predicted the great war in heaven, when the Vanir and the Aesir would begin a civil war that would bring down the walls of Asgard.

'Our meat is uncooked,' Odin said helplessly, pointing to the fire.

'The meat will remain uncooked,' said the eagle, 'until I ordain it to be cooked.'

The three travellers looked at the eagle with interest. It was not often that gods were challenged, and they waited to hear the reason.

'All right, then,' said Odin fairly, 'please could you allow our meat to cook.'

'I shall do so,' said the eagle, 'if I can eat my fill before you partake from the ox.'

Odin nodded and agreed, for he was famished by hunger now and he was determined to have some of this fine piece of ox. Within five minutes the beef was cooked, and with a flurry of feathers, the eagle landed by the fire and stirring up a great cloud of ashes, began to eat. Moments later there was silence. The eagle had returned to the tree, and the spit was empty.

Now Loki in particular was enraged by this act. He was accustomed to being the trickster, and was not used to having tricks played on him — whatever the reason. 'Who are you,' he called out angrily, to which the eagle only laughed and shrugged.

Loki grabbed a burning log from the fire, and made towards the eagle, who only ducked and dove at Loki until he was quite reddened with fury. Finally, the eagle swooped down and took in his talons the log which Loki held, drawing it up into the air as he flew. Loki struggled to let go of the wood, but he was unable to free himself. His fingers clutched the branch and nothing he could do would loosen them.

'Let me down,' he cried, angrily kicking his feet and shouting. But the eagle flew higher and higher, turning and soaring through the air and terrifying Loki so that he closed his eyes in fear. When at last the eagle sensed that his prisoner could take no more, he spoke.

'I am Thiazzi, the great giant. I will let you loose only if you swear to deliver the goddess Idunn to me. You must lure her beyond the walls of Asgard where I can catch her, and she must bring with her the basket of apples.'

Opposite:
The eagle flew higher and higher into the deep blue sky, turning and soaring through the air and terrifying Loki so that he closed his eyes in fear.

Loki considered this for a moment, and then agreed. Far below him Odin and Hoenir watched, never imagining the treachery of which Loki was capable. In a moment, Loki was set safely on the ground, and for a moment he sat there, stunned. Odin and Hoenir reached his side, and asked him what had passed with the eagle, but Loki told them nothing. The three men returned to Asgard.

Loki knew that the promise he had made to Thiazzi was the worst he could possibly have made, for without the golden apples of Idunn, the ravages of time would take their toll on the occupants of Asgard and he, Loki, alone would be responsible for the ageing and eventual death of each and every one of them.

He paced and paced the gardens where Idunn worked happily, her sweet ways bringing a nuance of spring to all she touched. But as much as Loki realized the trouble he would cause by luring Idunn from Asgard, he knew there would be much more trouble if he did not satisfy his solemn oath to Thiazzi. And so it was on that fateful day that Loki approached Idunn, who was curled up by a bed of flowers.

Idunn smiled innocently at Loki, and began to explain how the flowers responded to her love, and how all growing things could benefit from praise and care.

Loki smiled briefly and interrupted.

'Come, Idunn,' he said carelessly. 'Did you know that yesterday when I walked with Odin and Hoenir I saw a tree bearing enchanted apples just like your own.'

Idunn laughed. 'Why that's not possible,' she said brightly, knowing that her own golden apples were unique. They did not come from any tree, but appeared magically in her basket. When one was eaten, another quickly took its place so that there was an eternal supply of youth.

But Loki talked and talked to Idunn, and he managed to convince her that another source of apples would be a fine thing, for what should transpire if something were to happen to Idunn's basket?

'Bring your basket,' he said slyly, 'and you'll see that the apples are much the same.'

Idunn finally agreed to travel with Loki to see the tree, and they set out for the walls of Asgard. No sooner had Idunn stepped outside when Thiazzi swept down and clutching her in his talons, carried her away. With her went her basket of apples.

Loki skulked back inside the walls of Asgard, and mentioned nothing of what had happened. Soon it was discovered that Idunn was missing, and the Aesir became greatly distressed. Within a few days wrinkles appeared on their youthful cheeks, and their backs became hunched with age. They hardly recognized one another and as the bloom of youth disappeared, so did their happiness. Asgard was a changed place, and everyone called out for the return of Idunn.

Heimdall admitted that he had seen Idunn with Loki, on the fateful day of her disappearance, and at once Odin and his men set out to find the trickster. Loki admitted what had happened and the rage of Odin was so great that Loki volunteered to see about the return of Idunn himself.

Loki sat alone, deeply concerned by the task that lay ahead of him. For how was he to travel to the skies where Thiazzi lived as an eagle? Loki could take many forms when the need arose, but he had not yet mastered the art of flying, and he found himself in a quandary which even his quick wits could not find a way out of. Suddenly it came to him – Freyia's coat! Freyia's coat of feathers!

Freyia agreed at once to the loan of her hawk coat, for she was frightened by the wrinkles which cut deeply into her face and without her legendary beauty she would never be able to attract the souls of the warriors to her domain. And so Loki set out wearing Freyia's coat, and he flew at once over the walls of Asgard until he found the giant's castle.

There, in a pen, sat Idunn, and she was alone. Thiazzi's daughter Skadi had been watching the goddess, but because she was so serene and presented no threat of escape, Skadi had gone off for a walk, leaving Idunn to sit quietly, clutching her basket of apples.

Loki swooped down and spoke quietly to Idunn. 'Idunn, it's me, Loki,' he said quickly. 'Listen carefully: I am here to rescue you. In a moment you must hold your basket to you and I will turn you into a hazelnut and lift you into the sky and back to Asgard.'

Ever trusting, Idunn nodded her head and soon found herself high in the air with Loki the hawk. Just at that moment, Skadi returned and it took her no time at all to realize what had happened. She called out to her father, who was fishing several miles away, and he returned at once, rowing like a crazed person in order to reach his daughter. At once he saw Loki carrying away the nut, and he transformed himself into the giant eagle in order to give chase.

Loki was within reach of the gates of Asgard when the eagle approached. From Asgard the gods watched with horror, and Freyia cried out, 'My hawk will never outfly an eagle.'

And so the gods got to work, and directed by Tyr they put together a great pile of wood shavings which they set alight. Tyr held up the burning shavings and as the eagle flew across, he touched it to him, and the giant bird burst into flames, his feather coat melting off until the giant fell helplessly to the ground, where he was burnt in a rush of flames. There beside him stood Loki, trembling and frightened, but complete, and there was Idunn, mercifully unharmed by the chase, and by the blast of flames. She carefully handed each of the Aesir an apple, and youth was once more restored.

Just as the gods began to settle back into their daily routines, there came a shriek from the walls. There stood Skadi, crying out for her father who was nothing more than two burning embers. She cried out for vengeance, but Odin approached her and settled her down, pointing out that it had been her father who had begun this unhappy episode. It was finally agreed that Skadi would choose a god as her husband, in order that she would have a man to take care of her. She was to choose the one she wanted by looking at his feet.

So a screen was erected and each man in Asgard was bidden to walk past the screen so that she could see their feet. Choosing those that were the cleanest, and purest white, Skadi looked smug, sure that she had picked Balder, for no one else could have such clean white feet.

But when the screen was removed, there was Niord, god of the sea, whose feet were washed clean on the sands of the ocean each day. And so it was that the girl of the mountains married the god of the sea, and the two came together for all eternity. Thiazzi's embers were carried to the sky by Loki in Freyia's coat, and there they sit today, the twin stars of Thiazzi which bear his name and appear each night in the Northern skies.

Sigurd

First wilt thou prince,
Avenge thy father,
And for the wrongs of Eglymi
Wilt retaliate.
Thou wilt the cruel,
The sons of Hunding,
Boldly lay low:
Thou wilt have victory.

LAY OF SIGURD FAFNICIDE

ONCE, IN THE HALL OF THE VOLSUNGS, the great line of warriors who are celebrated in the great Scandinavian epic, the Volsung saga, a wedding took place. This was the wedding of Signy, who was to marry the king of Gothland, called Siggeir. Signy was the twin sister of Sigmund, who supported her marriage along with everyone in the kingdom. In the hall of the Volsungs was an unusual sight — built into the hall itself was a huge living oak tree whose branches supported the roof. This oak tree was called Branstock, and it brought good luck to the Volsungs, who tended it carefully.

On this day, the day of the wedding feast, there were great festivities underway. Great platters of food groaned on tables, and mead was passed around in horns as the joyful crowd toasted the health of the new couple. Suddenly there was silence, for in the midst of the crowd appeared a stranger with a wide-brimmed hat. He had only one eye, and his feet were bare and dirtied from his travels. In his hand he carried a spectacular sword, which glinted and shone in the light as if it were made of pure gold. He walked purposefully towards Branstock, and plunged the sword into the trunk of the tree without murmuring a word.

Then he turned, and addressed the crowd:

'Whosoever draws this sword from the tree will have it as a gift from me. Whosoever has as his own my sword will have victory in every battle he fights.' With that the stranger left the room, and there was silence. There was no doubt in any one of their minds that the great Odin had been amongst them.

Each of the men in the group stood up, longing for a chance to pull out the sword. Every great Viking warrior took his turn, while the others chattered excitedly. But one by one they pulled, and tugged and yanked at that sword until there was only one man left amongst

Opposite: Freyia agreed at once to the loan of her hawk coat, for she was frightened by the wrinkles which cut deeply into her face and without her legendary beauty she would not attract the warrior souls.

them – the small, fair young Sigmund. He stood and walked towards the sword, the room growing silent. Each of King Volsung's nine sons had failed as had the king himself. No one doubted that this young man would do so as well.

Sigmund laid his hands on the hilt of the sword and with a mighty pull, brought it from the trunk of the tree with ease.

This sword became Sigmund's property and as he grew older, he used it often, becoming the greatest Viking warrior that ever was. And then the day came when Sigmund had reached the final years of his life. He lay dying on a field, the last of the Volsung line, and as he spoke his final words, his beloved wife Hiordis bathed his face and wept over her dear husband.

'I have met with Odin once again,' he whispered to Hiordis. 'I know it was he because my sword could not match the mighty spear he carried. He has come to bring me to Valhalla, and dear one I am ready to go.'

He held out a weary hand and brushed away Hiordis's tears. 'Fear not, little one,' he said quietly, 'for in your womb you carry my son, and he will be the greatest warrior ever known – greater still than any Volsung. He will take my sword, and he shall reign supreme.' And then Sigmund died, as the Valkyrs led him gently to his peace.

Hiordis went on to marry the son of the King of Denmark, a man called Alf, who did not know that the child she carried belonged to Sigmund. When she gave birth there were great festivities, and the boy who was born was called Sigurd.

It is here that this story joins another, for once, just three or four years before Sigurd became a youth, and an apprentice to a smithy, Odin, Hoenir and Loki were walking in Midgard when they came across a burbling stream, rich with salmon and other fine fish. As they prepared to catch one for their meal, they were startled by the movement of an otter, who was just wakening at the side of the stream. Quickly Loki grabbed the otter and killed it, and a fire was quickly built while the otter was skinned. The men dined greedily, and with the pelt of the otter over their backs, they made their way towards a cabin, which was just peeking from between the trees. They knocked at the door and were startled to be met by an angry man who was summoning his thralls to help him tie up the three strangers.

Odin stepped forward. "Do you not know that passers-by are to be treated with kindness, and given a bed for the night? Do you not know that Odin has decreed this?' Odin was in his customary disguise and the angry stranger had no idea who he was dealing with.

Opposite:
The beautiful world of Asgard, guarded at the base of Yggdrasill by the Norns, would be threatened if Odin did not comply with Kreidmar's request.

The stranger, whose name was Kreidmar, scowled at Odin and said, 'Not when they have murdered my son.'

Kreidmar's son had been a form-shifter, and had just finished a fine meal of salmon, which he had caught in the shape of an otter. He had been murdered before he could become a man again.

Loki and Odin apologized profusely, and offered to do anything in their power to repay Kreidmar.

'There is only one thing you can do,' said Kreidmar, 'and that is to fill my son's otter pelt with gold, and then cover every hair on its back until I cannot see it at all.'

The three men agreed, and set out at once for a waterfall where they knew that a dwarf by the name of Andvari lived as a sharp-toothed pike and guarded a magnificent treasure of gold and jewels. With characteristic cunning, Loki managed to divert the fish, and as Andvari was changed back into a dwarf, to retrieve the treasure.

Loki and Odin gathered together the splendid gold broaches, rings, necklaces and ornaments, and as they made to leave, they saw something glinting from the pocket of the trembling dwarf.

'What's that?' said Loki, ever quick of eye.

'Oh, this ...' said Andvari, ' ... this you cannot have. This ring has a curse on it. Whoever owns it once it leaves my care will have nothing but disaster.'

Loki had little fear of curses and enchantment, for he could rival the best with his own, and he snatched the ring from the dwarf and the three men made their way back to the cabin. There they stuffed the pelt of Kreidmar's son, and then covered the body with more gold. Finally they were finished.

Kreidmar came to inspect. 'Ha!' he cried at once. 'I see a whisker still uncovered. You have failed in your task and I will kill you all.'

Loki stepped forward and bent down on his knee. 'Please sir,' he said graciously. 'I have this one ring here which will cover the hair, but it holds an evil curse and I do not wish it upon you or your family.'

'Give me the ring,' snarled Kreidmar, 'and all of you – be off!'

Opposite:
A few days later, he murdered his father and changing shape he became a monstrous dragon, hiding himself away in a fiery cave.

The three travellers continued on their way and soon forgot about Kreidmar and his son, but just moments after they left, the curse began to take effect. Kreidmar had two more sons, one called Fafnir, who also changed shape, and another called Regin. Regin was away, working as a blacksmith in Denmark, and he had as his pupil

none other than Sigurd, son of Sigmund. Fafnir, however, lived at home, and on the very day that the curse fell upon his father, Fafnir took on a peculiar glint in his eye and began to covet the treasure that filled his brother's pelt.

A few days later, he murdered his father, and changing shape, he became a monstrous dragon, hiding himself away in a cave and guarding his magnificent treasure.

Now Regin, far away from the treasure had, as part of the curse, begun to covet it himself, and he began to hatch a plan to have it returned. He assessed the young Sigurd, who was working with him, and noticing his bravery and his amazing skill with arms, he decided to approach him to see if he would fight the dragon.

'Sigurd,' he said slyly, ' I notice that you have come of an age that you may want to practise some of your great father's skills. There is a dragon I know of, one who guards a treasure. Perhaps you would like to test those skills?'

Now Sigurd was just young enough to be tempted by the idea of fighting a dragon for treasure, and he went off into the forest the following day to find a horse. As he walked through the trees, where the horses ran free, he met an elderly man, one with just one eye, who suggested that Sigurd test the horses before he made his selection. And so together Sigurd and the old man sent the horses into a nearby river. All of the horses swam easily to the other side, and then galloped off into the distance. Only one horse returned – a lustrous grey stallion with a powerful body and fine, intelligent eyes.

'Take that horse,' said the old man. 'He is a descendant of Odin's own horse, Sleipnir, and he will care for you in times of trouble.'

With that the old man disappeared, leaving Sigurd in no doubt as to who he had just seen. Turning to the horse, he stroked it and was rewarded by a happy snort. 'I'll call you Grani,' he said to the horse, 'and together we shall kill a dragon.'

Sigurd returned to Regin to tell him of his new horse, and to request that the blacksmith make him a great sword with which to kill the

Opposite: Sigurd did as he was bid, and he struck the great dragon, slaying him at once. He cut a hole in the dragon's neck, and then he bathed in the dragon's blood.

dragon. Regin began working, toiling over the hot forge until a sword was brought forth, gleaming. Sigurd lifted it into his hands, and then laid a heavy blow on the anvil. The sword broke into thousands of tiny pieces, and Regin looked at Sigurd in surprise. Back he went to the forge once again, and another sword was made, this one stronger and with a

gleam that was even brighter than the first. Again, Sigurd lifted the sword and brought it down on the anvil, and again, it shattered into tiny pieces.

Regin shook his head, and began work on a third. 'Go home, Sigurd, I will have another for you to try tomorrow.'

Sigurd was puzzled by the course of events, and a seed of doubt had entered his mind about the ambitions of his tutor. Regin seemed very keen to have the dragon slain, and Sigurd wondered why. He approached his mother and explained the whole story to her.

Hiordis said, 'My son there is a secret of which you are not aware. You are not the son of the man you think your father. You are the son of King Sigmund, and just before he died, he presented me with the pieces of this sword, which you may have forged to protect you. This sword will slay your dragon, if that is what you wish, and this same sword will protect you from whatever Regin has in store for you.'

The following day, Sigurd returned to the smithy with the sword, and it was placed in the fire by Regin. Suddenly there was a flash of bright light and the sword emerged of its own accord, glittering in the firelight like a crystal. Sigurd reached for the sword and brought it down on the anvil. At once the anvil split in two and the gleam was reflected in the eyes of Regin. He could think of nothing now but the treasure, and so it was that the two gentlemen set off.

When they reached the cave of the dragon, Regin said to Sigurd, 'Go on now, Boy, and slay the dragon. There will be treasure for us both. Whatever you do, don't let his blood touch you for you will burn for certain.'

Sigurd set off in the direction of the dragon, and as he approached, the stranger from the woods appeared to him once again.

'Sigurd, what Regin tells you is wrong. Bathe in the blood of the dragon, for it will make you invincible. Approach him from the back for if you go this way you will surely be burned.' With that the one-eyed man disappeared.

Sigurd did as he was bid, and he struck the great dragon from behind, slaying him at once. He cut a hole in the dragon's neck, and stripping off his clothes, he bathed in the dragon's blood until every part of his body was covered except for a tiny spot between his shoulderblades where a piece of heather had rested.

Gathering up the treasure, he returned to Regin who was delighted to hear of the spoils. 'Do me one more favour, Sigurd,' he asked, 'cut out the heart of the dragon so that I may eat it, and a part of my brother may live on in me.'

Sigurd returned to the dragon and did as he was asked. As he roasted the heart over a fire, a drop of the blood fell on to his hand, where it burned and began to smoke. Suddenly he began to hear voices. Looking around he saw no people, but the voices persisted. And it was at that moment that Sigurd realized that he could hear the birds speaking to one another, and they were discussing him! Sigurd listened while they spoke of Regin's treachery and how foolish he was to have trusted him. And when Sigurd looked up, there was Regin, ready to strike him down. With his mighty sword, Sigurd beheaded the blacksmith with one swing.

And so it as that Sigurd gathered up the treasure. As he put the same cursed ring in his pocket, he heard the birds say, 'He must not take the cursed ring. Does the great Sigurd not know what will happen if he does?'

But shrugging their words aside, Sigurd made off for home. As he travelled, he saw in the distance a fine castle, surrounded by white light. He coaxed Grani up and over the light, and he landed on the marble flagstones of the castle courtyard. Dismounting, Sigurd laid down his sword and entered the castle. There, in the main hallway, lay a knight in shining armour. Sigurd quietly reached towards the knights helmet, and lifted it gently off, curious to see what great warrior lay there in state. But to his great surprise, a tumble of hair fell out from beneath the helmet and there lay an exquisite girl. He prodded her, and as if by magic her armour disappeared, and her eyes opened.

When this girl caught eyes with Sigurd there came between them a feeling that happens most infrequently; it was a love with such intensity that Sigurd knew at once that she was a part of him, and he her. He slipped his hand into his pocket and withdrew the ring, slipping it on her finger. Some say this girl was called Brunhilde, and that she was the daughter of Odin. Other say she was born of Sigurd's need, and therefore was, in truth, a part of himself. Whoever she was, she became a part of Sigurd's life, and a part of the curse that he had just placed on her slender finger. But that, and the other tales of Sigurd and his adventures, is another story.

✳   ✳   ✳

THE LEGENDS OF THOR

I am the Thunderer!
Here in my Northland,
My fastness and fortress,
Reign I forever!

HENRY WADSWORTH LONGFELLOW,
SAGA OF KING OLAF

HOR WAS ONE OF THE TWELVE principal deities of Asgard, and he lived in the splendid realm of Thrudvang, where he built a palace called Bilskirnir. Here he lived as god of thunder, and his name was invoked more than any other in the age of the Vikings. For Thor was the protector of the land, a fine figure of a man with glowing eyes, firm muscles, and a red beard that made him instantly recognizable. He became known across the worlds for his great hammer, Miolnir (the crusher), which had been forged by the dark elves. This hammer, together with Thor's strength and his terrible temper, made him the fiercest god of Asgard, and the personification of brute force. Thor was also god of might and war, and because of his popularity, he soon grew to embody the forces of agriculture, and became a symbol of the earth itself. He is remembered throughout the world on the fourth day of every week – Thursday, or Thor's day.

How Thor Got His Hammer

First, Thor with the bent brow,
In red beard muttering low,
Darting fierce lightnings from eyeballs that blow,
Comes, while each chariot wheel
Echoes in thunder peal,
As his dread hammer shock
Makes Earth and Heaven rock,
Clouds rifting above, while Earth quakes below.

J. C. JONES, *VALHALLA*

THOR WAS MARRIED TO SIF, whose long golden hair was her one great pride. It fell to her feet like a ray of sunlight, and it was the colour of ripe cornsilk in the summer fields. As she brushed it, it glinted in the light and became a symbol of great beauty across Asgard. One day, the glistening cascade of hair caught the eye of Loki, and he wondered then how he ever could have imagined living without it. He thought about that hair all day, and all through the night. And then, just as the moon reached her pinnacle in the midnight sky, Loki leapt to his feet and made for Sif's bedchamber, where he knew he would find her sleeping. The moon cast long shadows into the sleeping goddess's delicately furnished room, and it was easy for the fleet-footed Loki to steal in and set to work.

Loki crept to the side of Sif's bed and very gently, so that he did not disturb her, he withdrew a pair of great shears from his cloak and cut her long veil of hair from her head. Winding the tresses around his arm, he darted from the room once again, and there was silence. Until, that is, Sif awoke to discover the travesty that had occurred.

Her shrieks brought everyone in the kingdom running to her side, and Thor howled with such outrage that the entire kingdom of Asgard shook. It was not long before Loki was ferreted out and brought before the irate god. Thunder boomed in the sky as the shaking trickster fell to his knees before Thor.

'I beg you, Thor,' he cried, 'let me free and I will find a new head of hair for Sif – one that is even more beautiful than the one she has now. I'll go to the dark elves. They'll fashion one!' Loki's head bobbed up and down with fright and eventually Thor gave in.

'You have twenty hours to come forward with the tresses, and if you fail, Loki, you will be removed from Asgard forever.' Thor banged down a thunderbolt at Loki's feet, and the traitor scampered hastily away, hardly daring to breathe at his good fortune.

Loki travelled at once to the centre of the earth, down into the Svart-alfa-heim, where the wily dwarf Dvalin had his home. He threw himself on the mercy of the dwarf, and requested as well two gifts with which he could win the favour of Odin and Frey, who were bound to hear of the news and wish to punish him themselves.

Dvalin worked over the heat of his forge for many hours, and as he worked he chanted the words which would make all he forged the finest there was – for there are no arms as powerful nor as invincible as those fashioned by dwarfs. First he finished the spear Gungnir, which would always hit its mark. Next, he formed the ship Skiblanir, which would always find wind, on even the most silent of seas, and which could sail through the air as well as on water. The ship was folded carefully and placed in a tiny compass. Loki's eyes shone at its undoubted worth.

Finally Dvalin spun the most graceful of golden threads, and these he wove into a head of hair so lustrous and shining that all the dark elves gasped at its beauty. Dvalin handed it carefully to Loki, wrapped in the softest of tissues, and said, 'As soon as this touches your princess's head, it shall grow there and become as her own.'

Loki took all the gifts from Dvalin, who he thanked profusely, and feeling very pleased with himself he set off for Asgard with a skip in his step. His jauntiness attracted the attention of two dwarfs who sat by the side of a small cottage.

'Why do you smile so?' asked the first – for Loki's reputation had preceded him and the dwarfs were certain that his happiness could have no virtuous cause.

'Dvaldi,' boasted Loki, 'is the most clever of smiths – both here and in all the nine worlds.' And with that he held up his prizes for the dwarfs to examine.

'Pish,' said the first dwarf, who was called Brokki, 'my brother Sindri can fashion gifts that are far more beautiful than those – and sturdier too.' He paused, and then continued, leaning towards Loki who began to look rather put out. 'Our gifts would hold the magic of the very centre of the earth,' he whispered.

Loki choked, and then, recovering himself, immediately challenged the dwarf to prove his words. So confident was he of the gifts he held now that he placed a wager on his own head.

And so it was that Brokki and Sindri made their way into their smithy and began work on the hottest of forges. Sindri agreed to fashion the goods, on the condition that Brokki blew the bellows – a task which would prove difficult over the great heat that was necessary for Sindri to win the wager.

Sindri at once threw some gold into the fire, and left the room, eager to invoke the powers which would be invested in a great wild boar, which he had decided upon for Frey. Alone with the roaring fire, Brokki worked hard at the bellows, never pausing despite the tremendous heat. Loki watched from the window and as he observed the determination and strength of the dwarf he began to grow uneasy. At once, he decided that he must intervene and as quick as a flash of light he turned himself into a gadfly and alighted on the hand of Brokki, where he set in a stinger so deep that a rush of blood rose to the surface immediately.

Brokki cried out in pain, but he continued the bellowing, never missing a beat. Sindri returned to the room and drew from the fire an enormous boar, who they called Gulinbursti for its radiant gold bristles. This boar would have the strength of all other boars there were, but he would have the additional ability to shine a rich and powerful light into any part of the world in which he travelled. He was the perfect gift for the sungod Frey and nothing could match the brilliance of its light but the sungod himself.

So Sindri flung more gold into the fire, and instructed Brokki to continue to blow. Once again, he left the room to seek the necessary enchantment, and once again Loki took on the form of a gadfly. In an instant he had landed on Brokki's cheek and stung through the weathered skin until Brokki cried out and turned white with pain. But still he worked on, pumping the bellows until Sindri returned once more. And triumphant, Sindri drew from the fire a ring which he called Draupnir, which would become the very symbol of fertility – for on every ninth night, eight identical rings would drop from Draupnir, with powers to match.

The final gift was yet to be prepared, and this time Sindri threw iron on to the fire, leaving Brokki hard at work as he left to call upon the final spirits. Brokki's strength was beginning to flag, but his will was as strong as ever. He pumped away as the fire burned brighter and brighter until, suddenly, a horsefly lit on his neck and stung him with a ferocity that caused him to leap into the air, but still he did not miss even one pump of the bellows. Loki was becoming desperate. He

Opposite:
Loki travelled at once to the centre of the earth, down into Svart-alfa-heim, where the wily dwarf Dvalin had his home.

arranged himself on the forehead of the hapless dwarf and he stung straight into a vein on his forehead that throbbed with effort. He was rewarded by a gush of blood that streamed out into the fire and into the Brokki's eyes. The dwarf raised his hand for a split second to wipe aside the blood, but that moment caused damage that could not be erased. When Sindri returned and drew out the great hammer, its handle was short and ungainly.

Brokki hung his head in disappointment, but Sindri pointed out that the powers of the great hammer would more than make up for its small size. Indeed, he thought it might be an advantage, in that it could be neatly hidden in a man's tunic.

So Brokki gathered up the gifts and carried them outside to Loki, who accompanied the dwarf back to Asgard with his booty. Odin was given the ring Draupnir, Frey was given the boar Gulinbursti, and Thor was given the hammer, which they had named Miolnir – meaning invincible power.

Loki then presented Sif with her golden hair, and when she placed it upon her shorn head it latched itself there and began to grow in swirls and waves until it reached her feet once more – a shining veil of hair that shone more brightly than ever. Gungnir, the spear, was given to Odin, and the ship Skidbladnir to Frey. Each god was delighted with his gift, and there was much camaraderie as they slapped the backs of the dwarfs and the redeemed Loki. It was Brokki who put a stop to the celebrations when he stepped forward and explained the wager that had been made by Loki.

The gods looked at one another, and eyed their magnificent gifts. Although it was agreed that Sif's hair could not be more lustrous, or more beautiful, the gods announced that Brokki's gifts were the finest and the most magical – for the sole reason that Thor's great hammer was of such a magnificent size that it could be hidden away and used against the frost-giants at a moment's notice.

Loki's games had backfired, and he turned on his heels and fled before Brokki could undertake his part of the bargain and behead him! Brokki started in outrage and implored Thor to come to his rescue in catching Loki who was making away at all speed. Still smarting from Sif's agony, Thor threw out a lightning bolt and caught Loki by the ankles, returning him to face his fate at the hands of Brokki and his brother.

But when Loki was delivered to the dwarfs, Thor took pity on Loki and insisted to Brokki that he could have Loki's head but that he must not touch his neck – for the neck of Loki belonged to him, Thor. Of course there was no way to remove a head without touching the

Opposite:
Thor raised the mighty hammer in the air – it was of such a magnificent size that it could be hidden away and used against the frost-giants.

adjoining neck, and Brokki stomped around in fury before he came up with a plan which would serve him equally. Gathering his brother's great awl for the purpose, he punched holes along Loki's lips and stitched them together with an unbreakable cord.

It was many days before Loki's howls of pain ceased, and many more before he was able to unstitch the cord. Loki did not speak for almost one hundred days, as his torn lips were so painful he could not bear to move them. In time, however, Loki was able to speak once again causing Thor – and everyone in Asgard – to rue the day that the wager was broken.

Thor Goes Fishing

On the dark bottom of the great salt lake,
Imprisoned lay the giant snake,
With naught his sullen sleep to break.

OEHLENSCHLAGER, *THOR'S FISHING*

THOR WAS A GREAT TRAVELLER, and it was in his capacity of war god that he took it upon himself to keep an eye on the activities of the occupants of the other worlds. One day, bored of his battles against the giants, he decided to take on a more dangerous opponent – the world serpent, Jormungander. How he longed to have the horns and head of the great beast on the walls of his palace hall.

And so it was that Thor dressed himself one morning in the attire of a human, trimming and curling his magnificent red beard until he looked the picture of elegance and gentility. He left Midgard and sailed across the sea until he reached Jotunheim. He anchored his ship and with his belongings tied upon his massive back, he set off across the sandy shores. A day or two later, he reached the cabin of the giant Hymir, who was not pleased to see the unexpected visitor.

Hymir knew that customs called for him to welcome the seafarer, but he had lived alone for many years and he disliked company.

Opposite:
Thor dressed himself one morning, and then he left Midgard and sailed across the sea until he reached Jotunheim.

'There's no point in resting your head in this household,' he said curtly to Thor, 'for I am up at the crack of the early light to go fishing, and then for the remainder of the day I've to see to my herd.' Hymir was the owner of a magnificent herd of steer, and he tended them zealously, allowing no one to interrupt his duties. He hoped that

he would put off the unexpected visitor by being too busy to entertain him, or to provide him with a comfortable bed, but Thor was not to be dissuaded.

Continuing to allow the giant to believe that he was nothing more than a travelling man, Thor laughed and said that he would enjoy very much accompanying the giant on his fishing expedition, in the hopes that he would learn something from his skills. And so it was that Hymir grudgingly allowed Thor into his hut and showed him a room where he could lay his head.

The first light of morning found Hymir preparing to set out for the river, which roared along the bottom of his property towards the sea. He moved quietly so as not to waken the traveller – he had no interest in or intention of taking him fishing and he wanted to be gone before Thor wakened. Slipping silently from the cottage, he moved towards the cattle, which he planned to milk before setting out in his boat. He was dismayed to find Thor waiting for him, patiently stroking one of the cattle.

'You'll be fishing next, I imagine,' said Thor with a wide grin.

'I fish alone,' said Hymir curtly.

'I'd like to join you,' said Thor.

'No room for passengers,' said Hymir again, moving to work on the first cow.

'Not as a passenger,' said Thor with a smile, 'as a fisherman. I'll help you with the rowing.'

Hymir could see that Thor was intent upon joining him and so he nodded grudgingly and pointed towards the manure heap. 'Find yourself some bait then,' he said with a grunt.

Now Thor had seen the giant gesticulating towards the cattle, who lounged over the manure heap. With a mighty blow of his sword, he beheaded one of the finest steer and held it up to show Hymir, blood dripping down his arm. The giant could hardly control his rage – he had intended Thor to dig for grubs, not behead one of his sacred cattle – but he said nothing. I'll lose him at sea, he thought to himself.

Eventually the two men set out in the boat and they began to row. Hymir had noticed Thor's carefully curled beard and assumed he was not

Opposite: The giant Hymir was not pleased to see the unexpected visitor and he sat sullenly on his great chair when Thor insisted upon being provided with hospitality.

the most manly of men, perhaps unaccustomed to the rigours of fishing and farming. He was greatly surprised when Thor took the oars and rowed with splendid ease for hours without showing any sign of fatigue. At last Hymir begged him to stop, pointing out that the best fishing spots were around them.

But Thor carried on rowing, intent on reaching the place where the Jormungander lived. He rowed for an hour, and then Hymir leaned forward and put a hand on his oar. 'You must stop here,' he said, 'for we have reached the waters where the Jormungander swims. Any further and we will attract his attention and be his first meal of the day.'

Thor brightened at this news, and rowed steadily until he was certain they were in the waters of the evil serpent. Then he carefully chose the strongest of Hymir's rods and reels, and placing a line as thick as his forearm on the rod, he placed his tackle on the great hook and let it fall into the water. It was only moments before there was a stirring of the water, and Thor felt his rod being pulled from his grasp.

In the dark reaches of the sea, Jormungander had spied the head of the slain cattle, and taken it in one bite. Now the sturdy hook was trapped in his throat and he thrashed and shrieked as he tried to dislodge it.

Thor stood firmly in the boat, his determination making him strong. He called upon the divine powers that made him godly, and drew in the writhing beast as if it were no more than a fish on a simple rod. Hymir sat back aghast – he knew now that his passenger could be no man. He had never seen such strength, such resolve, and when the serpent was drawn forth from the water, spitting poison and snarling, he turned yellow and fell into a deep faint. For the Jormungander was a frightening sight to behold – with massive teeth, huge, bulging eyes, and a deathly odour that spoke of all who had fallen at his will. Thor held tightly to his rod, muscles groaning with effort. The huge body of the serpent lashed the water into a frenzied current and the boat tossed and tipped, water filling the bottom, and then emptying once again with each terrible wave that passed.

Hymir came to and could take no more. Swiftly he leant forward and grabbed his sharp knife, sawing through Thor's line with all the force he could muster. And then there was silence. The Jormungander slipped silently into the black depths of the sea and disappeared.

Thor's roar was heard far away in Asgard, and his fury caused a great storm to erupt. He had been just about to draw the beast into the ship when robbed of his quarry. The serpent would not be such easy prey from now on and this trip had been wasted. He snarled at the giant and with-drawing his hammer, gave him a blow that sent him flying into the icy waters, never to be seen again.

Some say it was a blessing that Thor did not catch the world serpent on that day, for a prophecy had been made that if ever the

Jormungander's tail were removed from his mouth, the perpetrator would suffer a curse that would hang over him until the rest of his days. Thor rowed steadily until he reached the shore, and within a day he was back in Asgard. He did not speak of the fishing expedition again.

Thor in the Hall of the Giants

The strong-armed Thor
Full oft against Jotunheim did wend,
But spite his belt celestial, spite his gauntlets,
Utgard-Loki still his throne retains;
Evil, itself a force, to force yields never.

R. B. ANDERSON, *VIKING TALES OF THE NORTH*

THOR HAD PLANNED ONE of his regular trips to Jotunheim, and he set out on this occasion with Loki. It had not been many months since Loki had shorn Sif's hair and Thor decided that it was safer for all if Loki was under his own keen eye. So it was that they set out in Thor's chariot, and as night fell, they came upon the hut of a peasant, where they requested a bed for the night.

The peasant lived in a small hut with his wife and two children, and although they did not have much food to spare, they offered it all to Thor, who ate greedily. It soon became clear that there was not anywhere near enough food for all, so Thor took his two goats from the stable where he'd put them for the night, and slew them, roasting them over the coals of the peasant's hearth until the succulent meat slipped from the bones. He threw down his cloak on the floor and requested that the bones be placed there.

The peasant and his family were in ecstasy, for it had been many months since they had tasted fresh meat. And so carried away was the peasant himself that when Thor looked away from his meal, he slyly cut into the bone of the goat leg he was eating and tasted the marrow. When the meal was finished, Thor wrapped up the bones and placed them outside the door, and the two gods settled down for the night.

When morning came, Thor opened the door, and pulling aside his cloak, set free the two goats which had been reborn. He noticed, however, that one of his goats was rather lame, and that his front right leg appeared to be damaged in some way so that he found it difficult to walk. Thor was furious that his commands had been so rashly disregarded, and he realized that he would have to leave the goat behind, for it was too lame to travel. He thrust his great hammer into the air and was about to slaughter the entire family, when the peasant crept forward and confessed that he had been the one to eat the bone. He begged Thor to show clemency to his family, and grudgingly Thor agreed to take his two children Thialfi, a strong young boy, and Roskva, a pretty girl, to be his lifelong servants, as repayment.

So the peasant was left with the goats, and the four set out on foot, the chariot left behind until the crippled goat could walk again. The countryside was cold and sparse; what water they could find to drink was tainted by the smell of giants, and Thor became ill-tempered. Eventually, night began to fall and they were forced to find a place in which to sleep. Ahead of them was a great hall, and they approached it thankfully, curling up in its centre to spend the night. They had not been sleeping for long when there was a great banging and the earth began to rock and shake. The peasant's two children moaned with fear, but Thor pressed his hands over their mouths and bid them to follow him into an alcove which lead off to the side of the hall. There they huddled, and at last slept.

When morning dawned, the four weary travellers made their way from the hall and stopped with a start. For there lay sleeping a giant bigger than any they had seen before. His snores laid flat the sparse vegetation, and the peasant's children hurled themselves behind Thor in fright. Eventually the giant opened one sleepy eye and caught sight of Thor and his party. He snorted and then sat up, speaking in a loud rumbling voice, 'So you are the ones who dared to make your camp in my mitten.'

Thor looked around in surprise, and his eyes settled on the great hall in which they had managed to find shelter. The hall was none other than the giant's mitten – the alcove had been the thumb! Thor stepped forward and identified himself, and in return the giant said his name was Vasti. Vasti seemed a friendly giant and he suggested that the two parties put together their provisions and travel on together. Thor agreed, for it would do them no harm to have the additional assistance of a giant should they encounter trouble on their travels. And so they set off, Thor, Loki and the children scuttling along in the giant's footsteps.

The day was long and difficult. Even the great Thor struggled to keep up with the immense strides of the giant, and when it came time to eat, and to rest, he was as grateful as the others. Vasti opened his sac and removed a large piece of meat, which he consumed in a few moments. He grunted and passed the sac to Thor, and then

Opposite:
For there lay sleeping a giant bigger than any they had seen before, and his snores laid flat the sparse vegetation.

turned on his side and fell into a deep sleep, his noisy snores disrupting the landscape once again.

Thor reached greedily for the bag. They had had no sustenance all day and all four of them were weak with hunger. He struggled with the cord, and stamped and shouted, but despite his greatest efforts he was unable to unfasten the knots tied by Vasti. Loki then took the opportunity to weave his own magic on the knots, but they remained tightly fastened. Loki and the children settled down to sleep, too cold and hungry to bother any further, but Thor was irate. The giant's snoring made it impossible to sleep, and he was more hungry than he'd been since the day of his conception. Finally, he lifted up his great hammer and banged it down with all the force he could muster, on the giant's head.

Vasti turned, and muttered, and called out in his sleep that the leaf which had dropped on to him was a nuisance, and then he fell back into a deep sleep and left Thor to gaze at him in astonishment. A few moments later, he tried again, this time invoking a series of enchantments to make his blow even more supremely powerful, and he hit Vasti upon the brow – deep enough that the hammer was imbedded in the giant's skull. Thor dragged it out and waited for the inevitable shriek of pain, but Vasti only turned again in his sleep, and complained about a bit of bark that must have fallen from the trees overhead.

Thor had never been so infuriated. Everyone knew that he was invincible, that his powers were stronger than any on earth, and yet, with his fine hammer, he was unable to make the slightest dent on the sleeping giant. He tried one last time, and when Vasti started only slightly, and suggested that perhaps an acorn had fallen upon his head, Thor gave up, and tried to settle down to sleep.

He slept not a wink that night, and when Vasti rose, early on the morrow, he was in a fiery mood. Vasti had gone as far as he could with Thor and his men, and he would be travelling on to his own home across the icy mountains. He carefully pointed out the way to the castle of Utgard-loki, King of the Giants. But before he left, Vasti spoke quietly to the travellers and told them that they would find giants even larger than he was at the palace. Perhaps they should turn back now, he suggested, for he could not guarantee them any safety if they went on alone ...

But Thor was too fractious to listen to his warnings, and they went on towards the palace. In a few short hours they had arrived. The tiny size of the gods meant that it was easy for them to slip between

Opposite:
Thor intended to visit the palace of Utgard-loki in order to commence a battle that would ring across all nine worlds; his plans were not to be.

the bars of the fence surrounding the castle, and soon enough they had made their way to the inner chambers, the sanctuary of Utgard-loki himself.

The king of the gods was, as Vasti had promised, larger than all giants and fierce of countenance and expression. He laughed uproariously when he saw Thor.

'We have heard tales of you, Thor,' he said, 'and we know who you are by that red beard of yours. We didn't expect you to be ... so ... so ... small.' And with that, he broke out into laughter again, sending Thor into spasms of anger.

'My size is of no importance,' he said stoutly, 'for I am capable of feats that men of all sizes would find impossible.' Loki, who had also suffered enough on their journey leapt forward in Thor's defence.

'We challenge you to beat our many talents,' he shouted. 'And to begin with, I challenge you to find someone in your ranks who can eat a meal more quickly than I can.' Now Loki was more than confident of winning such a feat for he had an appetite that was keener than most gods at the best of times – here he was virtually starving after two days without food.

The king nodded his head in assent, and signalled to his cook Logi to join them. The table was laden with platters of bones, gravy and huge slices of dripping meat. At the sound of the horn, Logi and Loki began to eat. Loki ate ravenously, devouring meat and gravy with gusto enhanced by the powers he had called down to help him. At the sound of the horn he stopped and looked around. The king pointed to the other end of the table, and Loki stopped in his tracks. For not only had Logi eaten all the meat and gravy at his side of the table, but he had eaten the bones, the platters and the table as well. Utgard-loki smiled contemptuously and with a wave of his hand dismissed Loki, who hung his head in shame.

Thor stepped forward next, and held up his hand for silence. 'I hereby challenge any man or giant to drink a greater draught than me – anyone at all,' he shouted.

A horn was dragged before Thor and Utgard-loki smiled once again. 'Your challenge, Thor, shall be met,' he said. 'You'll see before you a horn which can, by our champion, be drunk in one or two great swallows. Let us see you match that.'

So Thor placed his mouth around the great vessel, which stretched the entire length of the room, and drawing in a deep breath, he began to drink. He sucked in the liquid and after many moments without breathing, he stopped, and crept along the length of the horn

to see how deeply he had drunk. The horn was full. The level of the drink had not moved by even the tiniest percentage. Thor shook his head in amazement. He knew his capacity for drinking was greater than anyone's and yet he could not make any real dent in the contents of the horn. He swallowed again, and then spat on the floor. 'Salty,' he muttered to himself, and sat down.

Utgard-loki just nodded his head and said quietly, 'One would have expected more from Thor, would they not?'

Thialfi had enough of the taunting; he had grown to love Thor in the days they had been together and he leapt quickly to his defence, volunteering himself for a race with the quickest of the giants. So Utgard-loki put forward his quickest man, a young giant called Hugi. The two boys lined up, and the race began. It seemed that the first race had been a draw, for both men appeared to reach the finish line at the same moment. And so another race was called, and they lined up once again. As the bell went, and as Thialfi lifted his foot to set off in the direction of the finish, Hugi raced to the line and back. The race was over and this time there was no question of who had won.

'Well, well, well,' said Utgard-loki, roaring with laughter. 'There are not many tricks to your trade, are there Thor?' to which the angry god trembled, but said nothing.

'What do you say,' shouted Utgard-loki, winking furiously at the crowd of giants who had arrived to witness the spectacle, 'you try to raise our pretty kitty.' He pointed to a giant cat who reclined gracefully in the corner of the hall.

Thor's pride had taken a beating and he was determined to prove himself. Surely it could not be difficult to lift a cat? He strode purposefully towards the cat, who yawned and licked her paw before sitting up. He tightened his belt Megingiord, which made him stronger, and then he tugged and pulled at the cat with all his might. But only one paw was lifted from the ground, and despite his every effort he could not move her. The cat batted him playfully with the paw he'd managed to lift, and laid back once again, her tail flicking to and fro in the sunlight.

Opposite:
As Thor summoned up his rage, and prepared to bring an end to the sedate lifestyle of Utgard-loki, there was a rush of mist and the world of the giants was completely enshrouded.

Thor looked towards Utgard-loki and asked for one final challenge.

'Hmmm,' said the king, 'there is one person in my household who may be suitable to wrestle with you. May I introduce you to my nurse, the hundred-year-old Elli.' There was great laughter

amongst the crowd as Elli crept forth, hardly able to hold herself upright.

Thor moved quickly towards her, and pulled and shoved until Utgard-loki called for him to stop.

Thor swallowed with difficulty. He was bewildered and he was furious; he stared at Utgard-loki and said quietly, 'I have been beaten. Until this day I thought there was no one greater than I. You have shown me my place, and for that I must respect you.' Thor signalled to Thialfi and Roskva, and with Loki on one arm, they made to leave the hall, defeated and humiliated.

But Utgard-loki called out in a voice that was at once humane and conciliatory. 'You have come here today against my will,' he said proudly. 'This is our home and you are not welcome here. Your show of strength is not welcome here. I was forced to do something to keep you away forever.'

At that the giant transformed and in an instant he was Vasti. 'Do you recognize me?' he said. 'When I lay sleeping just last night, I took the precaution of placing a mountain over my head – one which was invisible to you, Thor. And it is just as well, for it seems that when you were unable to open the magic cord of my sac, you took it upon yourself to hit the mountain.' There he paused, and casting open a curtain, gesticulated out the window at a series of valleys surrounding the mountain on the horizon. 'Those valleys,' he said solemnly, 'are the blows you aimed to my head.'

Thor gasped, but said nothing, waiting for the king to continue. And continue he did. Loki's opponent had been none other than wildfire, and Thialfi's racing partner had been the king's thoughts – and there could be none as swift as these. Thor's drinking horn had been dipped at one end into the ocean, and no matter how deeply he had drunk, the ocean would have remained undrinkable. Utgard-loki commented that the tides of the ocean had been altered by Thor's great swallows, but then he hurriedly went on.

The cat was in reality Jormungander, the world serpent, and had Thor not heard the gasp of terror when it seemed as though Thor may be responsible for removing the serpent's tail from its mouth? Everyone there knew what chaos would exist when such an occurrence would happen, for it had been prophesied that the end of the world would be nigh.

Elli was old age itself, and he had nearly unseated her. In all, Thor had been successful in many ways.

'You may hold your head high,' said Utgard-loki proudly. 'But please, Thor, do not return to our shores.'

Thor was only slightly placated by the king's explanations, and he lifted his powerful hammer to bring to an end the sedate lifestyle of Utgard-loki and his men. But as quickly as he could lift his hammer, the castle was enveloped in a sea of mist, and he could see nothing. The world of the giants was completely enshrouded and Thor had no recourse but to return home to Asgard. His mission was incomplete, and Thor had been branded a puny weakling in the eyes of the giant, but he had faced many of nature's most formidable enemies and had left his mark. And for that the god of war could stand tall once again.

The Stealing of Thor's Hammer

Wrath waxed Thor, when his sleep was flown,
And he found his trusty hammer gone;
He smote his brow, his beard he shook,
The son of earth 'gan round him look;
And this the first word that he spoke:
'Now listen what I tell thee, Loke;
Which neither on earth below is known,
Nor in heaven above: my hammer's gone.'

HERBERT, *THRYM'S QUIDA*

THOR'S HAMMER BECAME A SYMBOL of his energy and power, and the mere mention of its name, Miolnir, was enough to send the giants of Jotunheim trembling. Its neat compact size allowed it to be hidden easily on Thor's person, and he never was without it – except on those nights that he shared his marriage bed with Sif. On one such occasion, after a long and happy night, Thor woke, and stretching out a lazy hand, reached for Miolnir.

It had vanished.

His cry of anger soon had all of the palace attendants at his side, and many fruitless hours were spent searching for the missing weapon. Loki was summoned, for matters involving theft – particularly in Thor's household – tended to have his hand in them, but his innocence was undoubted on this occasion, and he pledged to help Thor find the real thief.

Loki asked to borrow Freyia's hawk's coat, and after collecting it from Folkvang, he set off for Jotunheim, travelling across sea and barren stretches of land until he found what he was looking for – a giant was sitting alone on a crag. Now this giant's name was Thrym, and as prince of the frost-giants, he had cause to dislike and indeed fear Thor, who had made massive losses in their numbers with his great hammer. Loki settled himself beside the giant, and mustering up all of his wile, set about asking him questions. At last the truth was divulged – Thrym had stolen the hammer and had buried it in a secret location. He would not return it to Thor, unless … and here the great giant paused … unless Freyia was presented to him as his bride.

Loki let out a great guffaw! Freyia was the most beautiful of all goddesses – a prize sought after by gods, men and all other creatures alike. It was certainly unlikely that she would agree to marry this prince of giants. Loki told Thrym these things, but Thrym stood firm. He would return the hammer when Freyia was made his bride – this was his sole condition.

Loki thought hard for a moment, and then made a quick decision. He'd promise Thrym what he wanted, and then leave the matters in the hands of Thor, who would surely find a way round it all. With a smile he rose and indicated that Thrym's conditions had been accepted. The giant's smile was greedy, and he rubbed his hands together in glee as Loki disappeared into the morning sky.

Now Loki's journey took long enough for him to realize that Freyia was not going to be happy about the bargain he had just arranged, and he immediately regretted his hasty acceptance of the giant's proposal. Surely a man of greater wit could have concocted something more practical, he lamented as he flew. When he arrived, he cornered Freyia and spoke as quickly as he could, begging her to consider the proposal – for wasn't Thor's hammer important to all of them? Wasn't the very safety of Asgard at risk if he was unable to fight off the attacks of the frost-giants?

But Freyia was outraged at the suggestion that she marry a mere giant, and give up all the splendours of her home. She commanded Loki to leave her, and she shut the door smartly behind him. Loki returned to Thor with his head bowed low in shame. Thor listened carefully to his explanation, and patted the surprised Loki on the shoulder.

'You've done the best thing,' he said gently, much to Loki's astonishment. 'My hammer is the most important thing here.'

And so it was that Loki and Thor set out to beg Freyia to reconsider.

Opposite:
Loki changed forms several times in order to plead Freyia to travel with him to marry the prince of giants, but she remained firm.

They had underestimated the passion of her feelings, for she commenced a tantrum that lasted for one whole day and night – one so fierce that the necklace about her neck was splintered in to pieces that flew from one end to the other of Asgard. Thor and Loki realized that their attempts were useless, and returned back to Thrudvang.

There they sat and ruminated for many hours, eventually calling upon Heimdall to provide them with advice. His suggestions were met with outrage as profound as Freyia's own anger – for he believed that the very best way for Thor to retrieve his hammer was to dress himself in Freyia's necklace and wedding garments, and present himself as Freyia herself. Thor refused to consider such a plan, until it became quite clear that there were no alternatives. Grudgingly he agreed to don her clothes, and the necklace was secured from the many parts of Asgard and rebuilt to fit his own brawny neck.

Thor travelled with Loki to Jotunheim and with his eyes averted, and a veil covering the coarse red beard and hair, he was presented to Thrym. Thrym welcomed them at the palace door, and his anticipation of having the lovely Freyia as his bride caused him to lick his lips, and made his eyes water so that his eyesight was compromised. He looked slightly astonished by Freyia's size, but he accepted that gods were larger than humans, and that they were much closer to giants in that respect. He led Loki and Thor to the banqueting hall, where the women of the bridal party were taking a meal.

Thor sat down at the end of the table, and reached greedily for the platters of meat and bread. Within a few moments, he had eaten an ox, eight great salmon, and all of the sweet cakes and viands which had been prepared for the women. And this great meal was washed down with two full barrels of mead. Thrym gaped at the spectacle, and could only be comforted when Loki explained that the lovely Freyia had been unable to eat for nearly eight days in anticipation of their meeting.

Thrym gazed with great admiration at such an appetite, for such things were commended in those times, and caught Freyia's eyes. He started back at once, for there was there such burning fury that he felt as if he had been struck by a bolt of Thor's own lightning. He turned with dismay to Loki, but he was soon soothed by Loki's assurance that Freyia was so deeply in love with him that her passion had consumed her, and her look was one of intense longing.

Thrym gathered together the men and women in his party and called for the great hammer to be brought forth – a symbol of the sacred vows which were to commence. He took Freyia's hand, and was slightly disconcerted to discover that on its back were thick, curling red hairs. As he looked into his loved one's eyes, Thor struck. He grabbed his hammer and with one great burst of energy, he slew every giant in the room, and left the palace in ruins. And then, turning to the destruction, he called out a proclamation which caused Loki to stop in his tracks. Thor claimed the land as his own, and from every corner tender green shoots of grass and greenery began to grow. The barren wasteland was fertile; their journey had been a success.

So Thor removed Freyia's clothing, and returned to present the goddess of love with her necklace. The Aesir rejoiced at the return of Thor's hammer, and all was happy again in Asgard.

Opposite:
Thor left the palace in ruins, and, turning to the destruction, he called out a proclamation which caused Loki to stop in his tracks.

❋   ❋   ❋

FREYIA
AND OTHER STORIES

Freyia, thin robed, about her ankles slim
The grey cats playing.

WILLIAM MORRIS, *THE LOVERS OF GUDRUN*

REYIA CAME TO ASGARD from Vanaheim, and before long she was as beloved as if she had been born one of the Aesir. She married well, and brought forth many fine children. She was known particularly for her fine feathered coat, which allowed her – and those she permitted to borrow it – to soar through the air as a hawk. Freyia's story touches on those of many of the other gods, and there are other myths and legends which must be recorded in order to understand how the golden age of Asgard became what it was, how evil entered, and how it eventually fell. There is Niord, who came with Freyia to bring summer, once the seasons had fallen into place. And Tyr, the god of war, who showed bravery which far surpassed any shown by man or god in the heyday of Asgard. And in the stories that follow we meet the elves, and learn why they abandoned their happy existence deep in the bowels of the earth. For every tale leads towards a single inevitable event – Ragnarok, and it hovers at the edge of all, just as it did in those early days of sunlight, when darkness had not yet touched the world of Asgard, and the gods lived a life of splendour ...

Freyia

And Freyia next came nigh, with golden tears;
The loveliest Goddess she in Heaven, by all
Most honour'd after Frea, Odin's wife.

MATTHEW ARNOLD, *BALDER DEAD*

FREYIA WAS THE NORTHERN GODDESS of beauty and of love, a maiden so fair and graceful that the gods honoured her with the realm of Folkvang and the great hall Sessrymnir, where she would, in eternity, surround herself with all of those who loved her. Like many Viking goddesses, Freyia was fierce and fiery, her cool demeanour masking a passion which lay burning beneath. She was clever, and masterful in battle, and as Valfreya, she often led the Valkyrs to the battlefields where she would claim many of the slain heroes. She wore a simple, flowing garment, held firmly in place on her torso and arms with the finest shining armour, a helmet and shield.

Slain heroes were taken to Folkvang, where they lived a life such as they had never experienced on earth. Their wives and lovers came to join them and Freyia's reputation spread far and wide among the dead and the living. So luxurious was Folkvang, so exquisite were Freyia's charms that lovers and wives of the slain would often take their own lives in order to meet with their loved ones sooner, and to experience the splendour of her land.

And so it was that Freyia, gold of hair and blue of eyes, came to be a symbol of love and courtship, and through that, the earth – which, of course, represents fecundity and new life. She married Odur who symbolized the sun, and together they had two daughters, Hnoss and Gersemi, beautiful maidens who had inherited their mother's beauty, and their father's charisma and charm. But Odur was a man of wandering eyes, and one who appreciated the inner music of women – and not just that of his wife. He grew tired of her song, and her absorption with their daughters, and he grew restless and reckless. And after many months and then years of growing weary of the smiling face of his lovely wife, he left Freyia and his daughters and set off on travels which would take him to the ends of the earth, and around it.

Freyia sank into a despair that cast a shadow across the earth. Her tears ran across cheeks that no longer bloomed, and as they touched the earth they became golden nuggets, sinking deep into the

Opposite:

As Valfreya, Freyia often led the Valkyrs to the battlefields where she would claim many of the slain heroes.

soil. Even the rocks were softened by her tears which flowed without ceasing as she made her decision. And it was decided by Freyia that she could not live without Odur. As well as being the symbol of the summer sun, Odur represented passion and ardour. Without him, Freyia could no longer find it in her heart to bring love and affection to those around her, and she could not fulfil her duties as goddess of love. It was decided that she should travel to find him, so across the lands she passed, leaving behind her tears which glistened and hardened into the purest gold. She travelled far and wide, and took on disguises as she moved, careful to leave no clue as to her identity in the event that he should hear word of her coming and not wish to see her. She was known as Syr and Skialf, Thrung and Horn, and it was not until she reached the deepest south, where summer clung to the land, that she found Odur.

Her husband lay under the myrtle trees that lined the sunny banks of a stream. Reunited, they lay together there, warm in one another's arms and dusted with the glow of true love. And as the passion drew colour into the cheeks of his wife, Odur knew he had to look no further to find his heart's content. The trees above them cast their scent across this happy couple, endowing them with good fortune. They rose together then, and Odur and Freyia made their way towards their home, and their exquisite

daughters. As they walked, the earth rose up to meet them, casting bouquets of fragrant flowers in their path, drawing down the boughs of the flowering trees so they kissed the heads of the lovers. The air was filled with the rosy glow of their love, and everything living joined a chorus of cheers which followed their path. Spring and summer warmed the frozen land which had stood desolate and empty when Odur left.

The loveliest of the new flowers which bloomed were named 'Freyia's hair', and 'Freyia's eyedew' and to this day brides wear myrtle in their hair – a symbol of good fortune and true love.

Niord

Niord, the god of storms, whom fishers know;
Not born in Heaven – he was in Vanheim rear'd,
With men, but lives a hostage with the gods;
He knows each frith, and every rocky creek
Fringed with dark pines, and sands where sea-fowl scream.

MATTHEW ARNOLD, *BALDER DEAD*

WHEN THE WAR BETWEEN THE AESIR AND THE VANIR was concluded, and hostages were taken by each side, Niord, with his children, Freyia and Frey, went to live in Asgard. There Niord was made the ruler of the winds and of the sea near the shore, and he was presented with a lush palace on the shores of Asgard, which he called Noatun. Here he took up the role of protecting the Aesir from Aegir, the god of the sea, who had a fiery temper, and who could, at a moment's notice, send waves crashing upon the unprotected shores of Asgard.

Niord was a popular god, and he was as handsome as his children. On his head he wore a circle of shells, and his dress was adorned with fresh, lustrous green seaweed. Niord was the very embodiment of summer, and each spring he was called upon to still the winds and move the clouds so that the sun's bright rays could touch the earth and encourage all to grow.

Niord had been married to Mother Earth, Nerthus, but she had been forced to stay behind when Niord was summoned to become a hostage for the Vanir, so he lived alone in Niord, an arrangement which he did not mind in the least. For from Noatun he could breathe in the fresh salt air, and revel in the flight of the gulls and other

Opposite:
It was decided that Freyia would travel to find him, so across the lands she passed, often accompanied by the Valkyrs, in search of her husband.

seabirds that made their home on the banks. The crashing waves lulled him into a state of serenity, and with the gentle seals, he basked in the sunlight of his new home.

All was well, until Skadi arrived. Skadi had chosen Niord as her husband, because of his clean feet, and he had grudgingly agreed to marry her. There could not have been two more different beings, for Skadi was now goddess of winter, and she dressed in pure white, glittering garments, embroidered with icicles and the fur of the white wolf. Skadi was beautiful, and her skin was like alabaster; her eyes were stormy, and told of a deep passion which burned within her. Niord was happy to take her as his wife, although he longed for the days of solitude that his unmarried days had accorded.

And so it was that Skadi moved her belongings to Noatun, and settled in there. The first night spoke of the nights to come, for from that first instant, Skadi was unable to sleep a wink. The sounds of the waves echoed deep in her head, and the cries of the gulls wakened her every time she drifted into the first ebbs of sleep. So Skadi announced to all that she could not live with Niord in Noatun – he would have to return with her to Thrymheim. Niord was deeply saddened by this arrangement, for the sea was a part of him – food for his soul. He finally agreed to travel with Skadi to Thrymheim, where he would live with her for nine out of every twelve months.

It was many days before Skadi and Niord reached her home, high in the frozen mountains, where frost clung to every surface and the air was filled with the vapour of their breath. The wind howled through the trees, sending showers of ice to the ground below, where it cracked and broke into tiny, glistening shards. The waterfalls roared in the background, sending up spray that glistened in the sunlight. At night the wolves joined the fracas, howling at the icy moon. Niord was quite unable to sleep even one wink.

So an agreement was finally forged between the two – for nine months of the year, Niord would make his home with Skadi in the kingdom of winter. For the other three months they would return to Noatun, where he would invoke summer for everyone in Asgard. This arrangement worked well for many years, but both Niord and Skadi felt saddened by having to vacate their homes for months on end. Finally, despite their affection for one another, it was decided that they should part.

Skadi threw herself into hunting, honing her skills so that she became the finest marksman in the land. She married the historical Odin, and she bore him a son called Saeming.

Opposite: Skadi's home was high in the frozen mountains, where frost clung to every surface and the air was filled with the vapour of their breath.

Eventually, she married Uller, the god of winter and the perfect companion for the frigid goddess.

Niord returned to his palace by the sea, and frolicked there with the seals, who basked in the summer sun.

How Tyr Lost His Hand

Tyr: I of a hand am wanting,
But thou of honest fame;
Sad is the lack of either.
Nor is the wolf at ease:
He in bonds must abide
Until the gods' destruction.

SAEMUND'S EDDA

TYR WAS THE SON OF ODIN AND FRIGGA, queen of the gods. He is the god of martial honour, and one the twelve supreme deities of Asgard. He had no palace of his own, but he spent much time at Valhalla. Along with Thor, Tyr was the god of war and of courage, and he was invoked as patron saint of the sword. Tyr was distinguished by the fact that he had only one hand, and this is how it happened.

When Loki had run away and secretly married the giantess Angurboda, she bore him three horrible children – the wolf Fenris, Hel, and Jormungander, the world serpent. Loki was shocked by the appearance of these creatures, and he hid them carefully within Asgard so that no one knew of their existence. But eventually they grew to a size which made them impossible to confine, and when Odin discovered their presence in his kingdom, he took steps to rid Asgard of them forever.

Hel was flung into the depths of Filheim, where she would reign of the nine worlds of the dead. Jormungander was cast into the sea, where he grew to encircle the earth – biting his own tail to form a complete circle as the world serpent.

Opposite:
Niord returned to his ship and travelled to his palace by the sea, where he basked in the sun with the summer seals.

Fenris, however, was allowed to remain in Asgard, for Odin believed that an animal as beautiful as this would be capable of being trained, and perhaps growing to protect the inhabitants of his kingdom from attacks. None of the gods dared to go near him, and it looked as though Odin's plans would be impossible – when Tyr

stepped forward and volunteered to feed and tend to the angry wolf. A tentative relationship was established between the brave god and the wolf, and Fenris accepted food from Tyr, and allowed him to approach without eating him whole.

But like the world serpent, who grew to encircle the earth in just a few short months, Fenris soon reached a size that made it unsafe for any man or god to approach him. His size and strength had become frightening, even for the courageous Tyr, and so the council of Asgard met to discuss his fate.

The peace treaty which had been signed by all members of the council did not allow any blood to be shed on the shores of Asgard. It was therefore decided that Fenris should be bound by the strongest of cables, and kept as their prisoner until such time as they could work magic strong enough to control him.

The first chains were brought forth, and Fenris laughed out loud when he saw them. He held still as they were woven around his limbs, confident that he could burst them apart with one flex of his mighty muscles. His confidence was justified, for just seconds after the chains were locked, he released himself with ease.

The next chains were the strongest as any ever produced by gods, and they were duly wrapped around the heaving bulk of Fenris. Again, they were burst in one breath, and Fenris sat back and laughed at the sight of the puzzled gods.

And so it was that Loki was sent to the dark elves, where the dwarfs were requested to turn their magic to manufacture a binding that no man or beast could break. It was by magic that the silken rope was woven by dwarfs, formed from the sound of a cat's footsteps, a woman's beard, the spittle of birds and the longing of the bear. When it was complete, it was duly handed to Loki, who brought it to Asgard with a flourish. They named it Gleipnir.

Fenris looked carefully at the silken rope, and then shook his head. He would not allow himself to be wrapped in this cord, for although it seemed slender, and insubstantial, he had a deep instinctive distrust and he could not go against his nature. The gods surrounded him then, pleading that he hold still and test his strength against the slight bond of the cord.

Opposite:
As men, gods and elves alike cowered behind him, Tyr volunteered to place his hand into the enormous jaws of Fenris.

Fenris sat quietly, and then spoke, his words falling like stones around the assembled gods. 'I will lay still for the binding, if I have your pledge that no magic arts have been used in its manufacture.

As a symbol of your honour, I would like the arm of one of the gods to be placed in my mouth as you bind me.'

The gods looked at one another, and then at Fenris. There was no question but that magic had been used to produce Gleipnir – for it was the only way they would be able to make something strong enough to control the wolf. They began to draw back, admitting defeat, when the sturdy Tyr strode forward, and confidently placed his arm in the enormous jaws. The gods moved quickly, and fastened Gleipnir around Fenris's neck and paws, and when they were finished, and Fenris was quite unable to free himself, they shouted with pleasure. At that moment, the great jaws snapped down, biting the god's hand at the wrist and swallowing it whole.

Tyr took this maiming with dignity, and he learned to use the maimed arm as his shield and to wield his sword with his left hand. Fenris was taken to the boulder Thviti, which was sunk deep into the ground. There he let out such fearful howls that the gods were forced to take yet one more measure to silence him. Tyr himself forged a steel sword of intense strength and purpose, and he placed it into the mouth of the great wolf so that the hilt rested in the lower jaws, and the point rested in the top of his mouth. Fenris's efforts to dislodge it caused a stream of blood to surge forth, and this became the river Von.

Fenris remained there until the last day, and then he would burst forth to prowl the earth forever.

The Passing of the Dwarfs

Away! let not the sun view me –
I dare no longer stay;
An Elfin-child, thou wouldst me see,
To stone turn at his ray.

LA MOTTE-FOUQUÉ

Opposite: *The dwarfs became great friends to the gods, but when evil entered Asgard, the dwarfs lost interest in the world above and disappeared.*

WHEN THE EARTH WAS FORMED, the first dwarfs were bred from the corpse of Ymir. Dwarfs were also called black elves, and they were such ugly creatures that it was decreed that they should not be allowed to show their faces above ground, for fear of frightening gods and men to death. They were dark of skin, which made them nearly invisible in the dark, and they were never seen, for they risked being turned to

stone by appearing in the daylight. Dwarfs were fine craftsmen, and although they lacked the size and power of the gods, they were certainly more intelligent than any other form of life in the nine worlds, and they were called upon often by the gods to provide assistance when their own magic failed.

And so it was that the dwarfs became great friends to the gods, helping them out by producing the peerless ship Skidbladnir, the golden locks of Sif, the hammer Miolnir, the golden-skinned pig Gulinbursti, the ring Draupnir, the spear Gungnir, and Freya's exquisite necklace, Brisingamen. Without these aids, the gods would never have had the power to keep at bay their many enemies, and when the old gods finally succumbed, the dwarfs themselves lost interest in the world above, and disappeared. This was the passing of the dwarfs.

When the old gods were no longer worshipped in the north, the dwarfs formed a conference and it was decided that they could no longer offer any help to humankind. For centuries they had made themselves useful in households – appearing to knead bread, or help with the farming, or rock a baby when necessary. But the twilight of the gods had caused a change of heart. One night, the dwarfs hired a ferryman, and for the whole of that night he was kept busy, filling his boat with his invisible passengers, so that it nearly sank, and transporting them back and forth across the river. When his night's work was complete, he was rewarded with riches beyond his greatest imaginings. The next morning the dwarfs had vanished from the land of the dark elves, a cry of protest against the disbelief of the people. Left to his own resources, no man was capable of running a household as smoothly without the helpful dwarfs, and no weapon as wondrous or as

invincible as those formed by the dwarfs was ever produced again. The passing of the dwarfs marked the end of an age, and the end of the camaraderie between the two worlds.

Oberon and Titiana

Every elf and fairy sprite
Hop as light as bird from brier;
And this ditty after me
Sing, and dance it trippingly.

WILLIAM SHAKESPEARE,
A MIDSUMMER NIGHT'S DREAM

NO DISCUSSION OF THE ELVES, or dwarfs as they were commonly known, is complete without a few words about Oberon. There are stories told far and wide of the fairy king Oberon, and his delicate queen Titiania. Oberon was so exquisitely handsome, that mortals were drawn into his fairy world after just one glance at his elegant profile. In every country across the world, there was a sense of unease on the eve of Midsummer, for this is when the fairies congregate around Oberon and Titiana and dance. Fairy dances are a magical thing, and their music is so compelling that all who hear it find it irresistible. But once a human, or indeed a god, succumbs to the fairy music, and begins to dance, he will be damned to do so until the end of his days, when he will die of an exhaustion like none other.

Oberon was also very powerful, and his tricks above ground became legend throughout many lands. With the passing of the dwarfs, humankind had no help with their work, and the little folk were no longer considered to be a blessed addition to a household. Many believe that Oberon harnessed the powers of Frey when he fell, and used them beneath the earth to set up a kingdom of fairies which was as complex and commanding as Asgard had once been. With his strength, and his overwhelming beauty, he was considered by man to be nothing more than a demon.

Opposite: On the eve of Midsummer, the fairies congregate around Oberon and Titiana and dance. Fairy dances are a magical thing, and their music is utterly compelling.

✳   ✳   ✳

THE END
OF THE WORLD

We shall see emerge
From the bright Ocean at our feet an earth
More fresh, more verdant than the last, with fruits
Self-springing, and a seed of man preserved,
Who then shall live in peace, as then in war.

MATTHEW ARNOLD, *BALDER DEAD*

ALDER WAS PURE OF HEART, and he represented goodness in every form. His life in Asgard was one of kindness and generosity, and while he lived the force of his righteousness would allow everyone in Asgard to enjoy peace from evil. But evil comes in many forms and not even the gods could be protected from its sinister influence forever. In Asgard, Loki was the evil that would burst the bauble of their happiness, and it was Loki who would bring about the end to the eternal conflict between virtue and corruption. It was an end that had been predicted since the earth was created, and its reality was as frightening as every prediction had suggested. Ragnarok would rid the world of evil, and leave a trail of ashes that blotted out the sun and all that had once glowed in their gilded world. But it is from ashes that new life springs, and the world of the Viking gods was no exception.

The Death of Balder

So on the floor lay Balder dead; and round
Lay thickly strewn swords, axes, darts, and spears,
Which all the Gods in sport had idly thrown
At Balder, whom no weapon pierced or clove;
But in his breast stood fixed the fatal bough
Of mistletoe, which Lok, the Accuser, gave
To Hoder, and unwitting Hoder threw –
'Gainst that alone had Balder's life no charm.

MATTHEW ARNOLD,
BALDER DEAD

BALDER WAS THE BEAUTIFUL, radiant god of light and innocence. Each life that he touched glowed with goodness, and he was loved by all who knew him. His twin brother was Hodur, who was blind, and Balder tended to him with every kindness and consideration. Hodur worshipped Balder, and would do nothing in his power to harm him.

There came a morning when Balder woke with the dawn, his face tightened with fear and foresight. He had dreamed of his own death and he lay there petrified, aware, somehow, that the strength of this dream forecasted sinister things to come. So Balder travelled to see Odin, who listened carefully, and knew at once that the fears of his son were justified – for in his shining eyes there was no longer simply innocence; there was knowledge as well. Odin went at once to his throne at the top of Yggdrasill, and he prayed there for a vision to come to him. At once he saw the head of Vala the Seer come to him, and he knew he must travel to Hel's kingdom, to visit Vala's grave. Only then would he learn the truth of his favourite son's fate.

It was many long days before Odin reached the innermost graves on Hel's estate. He moved quietly so that Hel would not know of his coming, and he was disregarded by most of the workers in her lands, for they were intent on some celebrations, and were preparing the hall for the arrival of an esteemed guest. At last the mound of Vala's grave appeared, and he sat there on it, keeping his head low so that the prophetess would not catch a glimpse of his face. Vala was a seer of all things future, and all things past; there was nothing that escaped her bright eyes, and she could be called upon only by the magic of the runes to tell of her knowledge.

The grave was wreathed in shadows, and a mist hung uneasily over the tombstone. There was silence as Odin whispered to Vala to come forth, and then, at once, there was a grating and steaming that poured forth an odour that caused even the all-powerful Odin to gag and spit.

'Who disturbs me from my sleep,' said Vala with venom. Odin thought carefully before replying. He did not wish her to know that he was Odin, king of gods and men, for she may not wish to tell him of a future that would touch on his own. And so he responded:

'I am Vegtam, son of Valtam, and I wish to learn of the fate of Balder.'

'Balder's brother will slay him,' said Vala, and with that she withdrew into her grave.

Odin leapt up and cried out, 'With the power of the runes, you must tell me more. Tell me, Vala, which esteemed guest does Hel prepare for?'

'Balder,' she muttered from the depths of her grave, 'and I will say no more.'

Odin shook his head with concern. He could not see how it could be possible that Balder's brother would take his life; Balder and Hodur were the closest of brothers, and shared the same thoughts and indeed speech for much of the time. He returned to Asgard with his concerns still intact, and he discussed them there with Frigga, who listened carefully.

'I have a plan,' she announced, 'and I am certain you will agree that this is the best course of action for us all. I plan to travel through all nine lands, and I will seek the pledge of every living creature, every plant, every metal and stone, not to harm Balder.'

And Frigga was as good as her word, for on the morrow she set out and travelled far and wide, everywhere she went extracting with ease the promise of every living creature, and inanimate object, to love Balder, and to see that he was not injured in any way.

And so it was that Balder was immune to injury of any kind, and it became a game among the children of Asgard to aim their spears and arrows at him, and laugh as they bounced off, leaving him unharmed. Balder was adored throughout the worlds, and there was no one who did not smile when he spied him.

No one, that is except Loki, whose jealousy of Balder had reached an unbearable pitch. Each night he ruminated over the ways in which he could murder Balder, but he could think of none. Frigga had taken care to involve all possible dangers in her oath, and there was nothing now that would hurt him. But the scheming Loki was not unwise, and he soon came up with a plan. Transforming himself into a beggarwoman, he knocked on

Frigga's door and requested a meal. Frigga was pleased to offer her hospitality, and she sat down to keep the beggar company as she ate.

Loki, in his disguise, chattered on about the handsome Balder, who he'd seen in the hall, and he mentioned his fears that Balder would be killed by one of the spears and arrows he had seen hurled at him. Frigga laughed, and explained that Balder was now invincible.

'Did everything swear an oath to you then?' asked Loki slyly.

'Oh, yes,' said Frigga, but then she paused, 'all, that is, except for a funny little plant which was growing at the base of the oak tree at Valhalla. Why I'd never before set eyes on such a little shoot of greenery and it was far too immature to swear to anything so important as my oath.'

'What's it called?' asked Loki again.

'Hmmm,' said Frigga, still unaware of the dangers her information might invoke, 'mistletoe. Yes, mistletoe.'

Loki thanked Frigga hastily for his meal, and left her palace, transforming at once into his mischievous self, and travelling to Valhalla as quickly as his feet would take him. He carefully plucked the budding mistletoe, and returned to Odin's hall, where Balder played with the younger gods and goddesses, as they shot him unsuccessfully with arms of every shape and size.

Hodur was standing frowning in the corner, and Loki whispered for him to come over.

'What is it, Hodur,' he asked.

'Nothing, really, just that I cannot join their games,' said Hodur quietly.

'Come with me,' said Loki, 'for I can help.' And leading Hodur to a position close to Balder, he placed in his hands a bow and arrow fashioned from the fleetest of fabrics. To the end of the arrow, he tied a small leaf of mistletoe, and topped the razor-sharp tip with a plump white berry. 'Now, shoot now,' he cried to Hodur, who pulled back the bow and let the arrow soar towards its target.

There was a sharp gasp, and then there was silence. Hodur shook his head with surprise – where were the happy shouts, where was the laughter telling him that his own arrow had hit its mark and failed to harm the victim? The silence spoke volumes, for Balder lay dead in a circle of admirers as pale and frightened as if they had seen Hel herself.

The agony spread across Asgard like a great wave. When it

Opposite:
Frigga pleaded with Hermod, the swiftest of her sons, to set out at once for Filheim, to beg Hel to release Balder to them all.

was discovered who had shot the fatal blow, Hodur was sent far from his family, and left alone in the wilderness. He had not yet had a moment to utter the name of the god who had encouraged him to perpetrate this grave crime, and his misery kept him silent.

Frigga was disconsolate with grief. She begged Hermod, the swiftest of her sons, to set out at once for Filheim, to beg Hel to release Balder to them all. And so he climbed upon Odin's finest steed, Sleipnir, and set out for the nine worlds of Hel, a task so fearsome that he shook uncontrollably.

In Asgard, Frigga and Odin carried their son's body to the sea, where a funeral pyre was created and lit. Nanna, Balder's wife, could bear it no longer, and before the pyre was set out on the tempestuous sea, she threw herself on the flames, and perished there with her only love. As a token of their great affection and esteem, the gods offered, one by one, their most prized possessions and laid them on the pyre as it set out for the wild seas. Odin produced his magic ring Draupnir, and the greatest gods of Asgard gathered to see the passing of Balder.

And so the blazing ship left the shore, with full sail set. And then darkness swallowed it, and Balder had gone.

Throughout this time, Hermod had been travelling at great speed towards Hel. He rode for nine days and nine nights, and never took a moment to sleep. He galloped on and on, bribing the watchman of each gate to let him past, and invoking the name of Balder as the reason for his journey. At last, he reached the hall of Hel, where he found Balder sitting easily with Nanna, in great comfort and looking quite content. Hel stood by his side, keeping a close watch on her newest visitor. She looked up at Hermod with disdain, for everyone knew that once a spirit had reached Hel it could not be released. But Hermod fell on one knee and begged the icy mistress to reconsider her hold over Balder.

'Please, Queen Hel, without Balder we cannot survive. There can be no future for Asgard without his presence,' he cried.

But Hel would not be moved. She held out for three days and three nights, while Hermod stayed right by her side, begging and pleading and offering every conceivable reason why Balder should be released. And finally the Queen of darkness gave in.

'Return at once to Asgard,' she said harshly, 'and if what you say is true, if everything – living and inanimate – in Asgard loves Balder and cannot live without him, then he will be released. But if there is even one dissenter, if there is even one stone in your land who does not mourn the passing of Balder, then he shall remain here with me.'

Hermod was gladdened by this news, for he knew that everyone – including Hodur who had sent the fatal arrow flying through the air – loved Balder. He agreed to these terms at once, and set off for Asgard, relaying himself and his news with speed that astonished all who saw him arrive.

Immediately, Odin sent messengers to all corners of the universe, asking for tears to be shed for Balder. And as they travelled, everyone and everything began to weep, until a torrent of water rushed across the tree of life. And after everyone had been approached, and each had shed his tears, the messengers made their way back to Odin's palace with glee. Balder would be released, there could be no doubt!

But it was not to be, for as the last messenger travelled back to the palace, he noticed the form of an old beggarwoman, hidden in the darkness of a cave. He approached her then, and bid her to cry for Balder, but she did not. Her eyes remained dry. The uproar was carried across to the palace, and Odin himself came to see 'dry eyes', whose inability to shed tears would cost him the life of his son. He stared into those eyes and he saw then what the messenger had failed to see, what Frigga had failed to see, and what had truly caused the death of Balder. For those eyes belonged to none other than Loki, and it was he who had murdered Balder as surely as if the arrow had left his own hands.

The sacred code of Asgard had been broken, for blood had been spilled by one of their own, in their own land. The end of the world was nigh – but first, Loki would be punished once and for all.

Revenge of the Gods

Thee, on a rock's point,
With the entrails of thy ice-cold son,
The god will bind.

SAEMUND'S EDDA

THE WRATH OF THE GODS was so great that Asgard shuddered and shook. As Odin looked down upon Loki in the form of the beggarwoman, and made the decision to punish him, Loki transformed himself into a fly and disappeared.

Although he was crafty, even his most supreme efforts to save himself were as nothing in the face of Odin's determination to trace him.

Loki travelled to far distant mountains, and on the peak of the most isolated of them all, he built a cabin, with windows and doors on all sides so that he could see the enemy approaching, and flee from any side before they reached him. By day, he haunted a pool by a rushing waterfall, taking the shape of a salmon. His life was uncomplicated, and although he was forced to live by his wits, and the fear of the god's revenge was great, Loki was not unhappy.

From his throne above the worlds, Odin watched, and waited. And when he saw that Loki had grown complacent, and no longer looked with quite such care from his many windows, he struck.

It was one particular evening that Loki sat weaving. He had just invented what we today call a fish net, and as he worked he hummed to himself, glancing every now and then from his great windows, and then back at his work. The gods were almost upon him when he first noticed them, and they were led by Kvasir, who was known amongst all gods for his wisdom and ability to unravel the tricks of even the most seasoned trickster. And as he saw them arriving, Loki fled from the back door, and transformed himself into a salmon, and leapt into the pond.

The gods stood in the doorway, surveying the room. Kvasir walked over to the fishing net and examined it closely. His keen eyes caught a glimmer of fish scales on the floor, and he nodded sagely.

'It is my assessment,' he said, 'that our Loki has become a fish. And,' he held up the fishing net, 'we will catch him with his own web.'

The gods made their way to the stream, and the pond which lay at the bottom of the waterfall. Throwing the net into the water, they waited for daybreak, when Loki the salmon would enter the waters and be caught in their net. Of course, Loki was too clever to be trapped so easily, and he swam beneath the net and far away from the part of the pond where the gods were fishing. Kvasir soon realized their mistake, and he ordered that rocks be placed at the bottom of the net, so that none could swim beneath it. And they waited.

Opposite:
Skadi caught a poisonous snake, and trapped it by its tail so that it hung over Loki's face, dripping venom into his mouth.

Loki looked with amusement at the god's trap, and gracefully soared through the air above the net, his eyes glinting in the early morning light. And as his fins were just inches from the water, and when he was so close to escape that he had begun to plan his celebrations, two firm hands were thrust out, and he was lifted into the air.

He hardly dared look at his captor, and he began to tremble when he saw that it was none other than Thor who had moved so swiftly to catch him.

'I command you to take your own form, Loki,' he shouted, holding tight to the smooth scales of the salmon.

Loki knew he was beaten. Quietly he transformed himself once again into Loki, only to find himself hung by the heels over the rippling waters. And as Thor raised his great hammer to beat Loki to death, a hand reached out and stopped him. It was Odin, and he spoke gently, and with enormous purpose.

'Death is too good for this rodent,' he whispered. 'Take him at once to the Hel's worlds and tie him there for good.'

And so it was that Loki was taken to Filheim, where Thor grabbed three massive rocks and formed a platform for the hapless trickster. Then, Loki's two sons, Vali and Nari, were brought forth, and an enchantment was laid upon Vali so that he took the form of a wolf and attacked his brother Nari, tearing him to pieces in front of his anguished father. Gathering up Nari's entrails, which were now endowed with magic properties, he tied Loki's limbs so that he lay across the three rocks, unable to move. The entrails would tighten with every effort he made to escape, and to ensure that he could not use trickery to free himself, Thor placed the rocks on a precipice. One false move and he would be sent crashing to his death in the canyon below.

Finally, Skadi caught a poisonous snake, and trapped it by its tail

so that it hung over Loki's face, dripping venom into his mouth so that he screamed with pain and terror. He began to convulse and was such a terrible sight that his wife Sigyn rushed forward and begged to be allowed to stay beside him, holding a bowl with which to collect the poison.

The work of the gods was done. They turned then and left, and Sigyn remained with her husband, ever true to her wedding vows. Every day or so she moved from her position at his side in order to empty her bowl, and Loki's convulsions brought an earthquake to Asgard that lasted just as long as it took her to return with her bowl. They would remain there until the end of time – for the gods, that is. The end of time was nigh, and it was Ragnarok.

Ragnarok

Brothers slay brothers;
Sisters' children
Shed each other's blood.
Hard is the world;
Sensual sin grows huge.
There are sword-ages, axe-ages;
Shields are cleft in twain;
Storm-ages, murder-ages;
Till the world falls dead,
And men no longer spare
Or pity one another.

R. B. ANDERSON,
NORSE MYTHOLOGY

THE END OF THE WORLD HAD been prophesied from its beginning, and everyone across the world knew what to expect when Ragnarok fell upon them. For Ragnarok was the twilight of the gods, an end to the golden years of Asgard, an end to the palaces of delight, an end to the timeless world where nothing could interfere. It was the death of Balder that set the stage for the end of the world, and it was Loki's crimes which laid in place the main characters. And when the action had begun, there was no stopping it.

When evil entered Asgard, it tainted all nine worlds. Sol and Mani, high in the sky, paled with fright, and their chariots slowed as they moved with effort across the sky. They knew that the wolves

Opposite:
The Aesir carried Balder's body towards the sea, where they set alight a ship which would become his burning funeral pyre. Loki had disappeared.

would be soon upon them and that it would be only a matter of time before eternal darkness would fall once again. And when Sol and Mani had been devoured, there was no light to shine on the earth, and the terrible cold crept into the warm reaches of summer and drew from the soil what was growing there. Snow began to drift down upon the freezing land, and soon it snowed a little faster, and a little harder, until the earth was covered once again in a dark layer of ice.

Winter was upon them, and it did not cease. For three long, frozen seasons, it was winter, and then, after a thaw that melted only one single layer of ice, it was back for three more. With the cold and the darkness came evil, which rooted itself in the hearts of men. Soon crime was rampant, and all shreds of human kindness disappeared with the spring. At last, the stars were flung from the skies, causing the earth to tremble and shake. Loki and Fenris were freed from their manacles, and together they moved forward to wreak their revenge on the gods and men who had bound them so cruelly.

At the bottom of Yggdrasill, there was a groan that emanated the entire length of the tree, for at that moment, Nithog had gnawed through the root of the world tree, which quivered and shook from bottom to top. Fialar, the red cock who made his home above Valhalla shrieked out his cry, and then flew away from the tree as his call was echoed by Gullinkambi, the rooster in Midgard.

Heimdall knew at once what was upon them, and raising his mighty horn to his lips he blew the call that filled the hearts of all gods and mankind with terror. *Ragnarok.* The gods sprang from their beds, and thrust aside the finery that hung in their bed chambers. They armed themselves and mounted their horses, ready for the war that had been expected since the beginning of time. They moved quickly over the rainbow bridge and then they reached the field of Vigrid, where the last battle would be fought.

The turmoil on earth caused the seas to toss and twist with waves, and soon the world serpent Jormungander was woken from his deep sleep. The movement of the seas yanked his tail from his mouth, and it lashed around, sending waves crashing in every direction. And as he crawled out upon land for the first time, a tidal wave swelled across the earth, and set afloat Nagilfar, the ship of the dead, which had been constructed from the nails of the dead whose relatives had failed in their duties, and had neglected to pare the nails of the deceased when they were laid to rest. As the wind caught the blackened sail, Loki

Opposite:
The ship of the dead was set afloat, and as the wind caught the blackened sail, Loki leapt aboard and took her wheel.

❦ 120 ❦

leapt aboard, and took her wheel – the ship of the undead captained by the personification of all evil. Loki called upon the fire-gods from Muspell, and they arrived in a conflagration of terrible glory.

Another ship had set out for Vigrid, and this was steered by Hrym and crewed by the frost-giants who had waited many centuries for this battle. Across the raging sea, both vessels made for the battlefield.

As they travelled, Hel, crept from her underground estate, bringing with her Nithog, and the hellhound Garm. From up above, there was a great crack, and Surtr, with sword blazing, leapt with his sons to the Bifrost bridge, and with one swoop they felled it, and sent the shimmering rainbow crashing to the depths below. Quickly, Odin escaped from the battlefield, and slipped one last time to the Urdar fountain, where the Norns sat quietly, accepting their fate. He leant over Mimir, and requested her wisdom, but for once the head would not talk to him, and he remounted Sleipnir and returned to the field, frightened and aware that he had no powers left with which to defend his people.

The opposing armies lined themselves on Vigrid field. On one side were the Aesir, the Vanir and the Einheriear – on the other, were the fire-giants led by Surtr, the frost-giants, the undead with Hel, and Loki with

his children – Fenris and Jormungander. The air was filled with poison and the stench of evil from the opposing army, yet the gods held up their heads and prepared for a battle to end all time.

And so it was that the ancient enemies came to blows. Odin first met with the evil Fenris, and as he charged towards the fierce wolf, Fenris's massive jaws stretched open and Odin was flung deep into the red throat. Thor stopped in his tracks, the death of his father burning deep in his breast, and with renewed fury he lunged at the world serpent, engaging in a combat that would last for many hours. His hammer laid blow after blow on the serpent, and at last there was silence. Thor sat back in exhaustion, Jormungander dying at his side. But as Thor made to move forward, to carry on and support his kin in further battles, the massive serpent exhaled one last time, in a cloud of poison so vile that Thor fell at once, lifeless in the mist of the serpent's breath.

Tyr fought bravely with just one arm, but he, like his father, was swallowed whole, by the hellhound Garm, but as he passed through the gullet of the hound he struck out one last blow with his sword and pierced the heart of his enemy, dying in the knowledge that he had obtained his life's ambition.

Heimdall met Loki hand to hand, and the forces of good and evil engaged in the battle that had been raging for all time. Their flames engulfed one another; there was a flash of light. And then there was nothing.

The silent Vidar came rushing from a distant part of the plain to avenge the death of Odin, and he laid upon the jaw of Fenris a shoe which had been created for this day. With his arms and legs in motion he tore the wolf's head from his body, and then lay back in a pool of blood. Of all the gods, only Frey was left fighting. He battled valiantly, and as he laid down giant after giant, he felt a warmth on the back of his neck that meant only one thing. The heat burned and sizzled his skin, and as he turned he found himself face to face with Surtr. With a cry of rage that howled through the torn land, and shook the massive stem of the world ash, Yggdrasill, Surtr flung down bolts of fire that engulfed the golden palaces of the gods, and each of the worlds which lay beneath it. The heat caused the seas to bubble and to boil, and there came at once a wreath of smoke that blotted out the fire, and then, the world.

At last all was as it had been in the beginning. There was blackness. There was chaos. There was a nothingness that stretched as far as there was space.

The End of the World

All evil
Dies there an endless death, while goodness riseth
From that great world-fire, purified at last,
to a life far higher, better, nobler than the past.

R. B. ANDERSON,
VIKING TALES OF THE NORTH

THE EARTH WAS PURGED BY THE FIRE and there was at once a new beginning. The sun rose in the sky, mounted on a chariot driven by the daughter of Sol, born before the wolf had eaten her father and her mother. Fresh green grass sprung up in the crevices, and flowers and fruits burst forth. Two new humans, Lif, a woman, and Lifthrasir, a man, emerged from Mimir's forest, where they had been reincarnated at the end of the world. Vali and Vidar, the forces of nature had survived the fiery battle, and they returned to the plan to be greeted by Thor's sons, Modi and Magni, who carried with them their father's hammer.

Hoenir had escaped from the Vanir, who had vanished forever, and from the deepest depths of the earth came Balder, renewed and as pure as he had ever been. Hodur rose with him, and the two brothers embraced, and greeted the new day. And so this small group of gods turned to face the scenes of destruction and devastation, and to witness the new life that was already curling up from the cloak of death and darkness. The land had become a refuge for the good. They looked up – they all looked way up – and there in front of them, stronger than ever was the world ash, Yggdrasill, which had trembled but not fallen.

There was a civilization to be created, and a small band of gods with whom it could be done. The gods had returned in a blaze of white light – a light as pure and virtuous as the new inhabitants of the earth – and in that light they brought forth our own world.

✳   ✳   ✳

GLOSSARY

Aesir   Northern gods who made their home in Asgard; there are twelve in number.

Alberich   King of the dwarfs.

Alf-heim   Home of the elves, ruled by Frey.

Allfather   Another name for Odin; Yggdrasill was created by Allfather.

Alsvider   Steed of the moon (Mani) chariot.

Alsvin   Steed of the sun (Sol) chariot.

Andhrimnir   Cook at Valhalla.

Andvaranaut   Ring of Andvari, the King of the dwarfs.

Angurboda   Loki's first wife, and the mother of Hel, Fenris and Jormungander.

Asgard   Home of the gods, at one root of Yggdrasill.

Augsburg   Tyr's city.

Balder   Son of Frigga; his murder causes Ragnarok.

Bestla   Giant mother of Aesir's mortal element.

Bifrost   Rainbow bridge presided over by Heimdall.

Bilskirnir   Thor's palace.

Branstock   Giant oak tree in the Volsung's hall; Odin placed a sword in it and challenged the guests of a wedding to withdraw it.

Breibalik   Balder's palace.

Brisingamen   Freyia's necklace.

Brokki   Dwarf who makes a deal with Loki, and who makes Miolnir, Draupnir and Gulinbursti.

Brunhilde   A Valkyr found by Sigurd.

Chaos   A state from which the universe was created – caused by fire and ice meeting.

Draupnir   Odin's famous ring, fashioned by Brokki.

Dvalin   Dwarf visited by Loki; also the name for the stag on Yggdrasill.

dwarfs   Fairies and black elves are called dwarfs.

Edda   Collection of prose and poetic myths and stories from the Norsemen.

Einheriear   Odin's guests at Valhalla.

Eisa   Loki's daughter.

Elf   Sigmund is buried by an elf; there are light and dark elves (the latter called dwarfs).

Fafnir   Shape-changer who kills his father and becomes a dragon to guard the family jewels. Slain by Sigurd.

Fates   Called Norns in Viking mythology.

Fenris   A wild wolf, who is the son of Loki. He roams the earth after Ragnarok.

Fialar   Red cock of Valhalla.

Filheim   Land of mist, at the end of one of Yggdrasill's roots.

Folkvang   Freyia's palace.

Frey   Comes to Asgard with Freyia as a hostage following the war between the Aesir and the Vanir.

Freyia   Comes to Asgard with Frey as a hostage following the war between the Aesir and the Vanir. Goddess of beauty and love.

Frigga   Odin's wife and mother of gods; she is goddess of the earth.

Fulla   Frigga's maidservant.

Garm   Hel's hound.

Geri   Odin's wolf.

Giallar   Bridge in Filheim.

Giallarhorn   Heimdall's trumpet – the final call signifies Ragnarok.

giants   Usually represent evil in Viking mythology.

Gladheim   Where the twelve deities of Asgard hold their thrones. Also called Gladsheim.

Gungnir   Odin's spear, made of Yggdrasill wood, and the tip fashioned by Dvalin.

Gylfi   A wandering king to whom the Eddas are narrated.

Hati   The wolf who pursues the sun and moon.

Heimdall   White god who guards the Bifrost bridge.

Hel   Goddess of death and Loki's daughter.

Hermod   Son of Frigga and Odin who travelled to see Hel in order to reclaim Balder for Asgard.

Hiordis   Wife of Sigmund and mother of Sigurd.

Hodur   Balder's blind twin; known as the personification of darkness.

Hoenir   Also called Vili; produces the first humans with Odin and Loki, and was one of the triad responsible for the creation of the world.

Hrim-faxi   Steed of the night.

Hugin   Odin's raven.

Hymir   Giant who fishes with Thor and is drowned by him.

Idunn   Guardian of the youth-giving apples.

Jormungander   The world serpent; son of Loki. Legends tell that when his tail is removed from his mouth, Ragnarok has arrived.

Jord Daughter of Nott; wife of Odin.

Jotunheim Home of the giants.

Kvasir Clever warrior and colleague of Odin. He was responsible for finally outwitting Loki.

Lif The female survivor of Ragnarok.

Lifthrasir The male survivor of Ragnarok.

Logi Utgard-loki's cook.

Loki God of fire and mischief-maker of Asgard; he eventually brings about Ragnarok.

Magni Thor's son.

Mani The moon.

Midgard Dwelling place of humans (our earth).

midsummer A time when fairies dance and claim human victims.

Mimir God of the ocean, the head of which guards a well; reincarnated after Ragnarok.

Miolnir Thor's hammer.

Modi Thor's son.

Munin Odin's raven.

Muspell Home of fire, and the fire-giants.

Nanna Balder's wife.

Narve Son of Loki.

Night Daughter of Norvi.

Niord God of the sea; marries Skadi.

Noatun Niord's home.

Norns The fates and protectors of Yggdrasill. Many believe them to be the same as the Valkyrs.

Norvi Father of the night.

Nott Goddess of night.

Oberon Fairy king.

Odin Allfather and king of all gods, he is known for travelling the nine worlds in disguise and recognized only by his single eye; dies at Ragnarok.

Odur Freyia's husband.

Ragnarok The end of the world.

Regin A blacksmith who educated Sigurd.

Sessrymnir Freyia's home.

Sif Thor's wife; known for her beautiful hair.

Sigi Son of Odin.

Sigmund Warrior able to pull the sword from Branstock in the Volsung's hall.

Signy Volsung's daughter.

Sigurd Son of Sigmund, and bearer of his sword. Slays Fafnir the dragon.

Sigyn Loki's faithful wife.

Sindri Dwarf who worked with Brokki to fashion gifts for the gods; commissioned by Loki.

Skadi Goddess of winter and the wife of Niord for a short time.

Skrymir Giant who battled against Thor.

Sleipnir Odin's steed.

Sol The sun-maiden.

Surtr Fire-giant who eventually destroys the world at Ragnarok.

Svasud Father of summer.

Thialfi Thor's servant, taken when his peasant father unwittingly damaged Thor's goat.

Thiassi Giant and father of Skadi, he tricked Loki into bringing Idunn to him. Thrymheim is his kingdom.

Thor God of thunder and of war (with Tyr). Known for his huge size, and red hair and beard. Carries the hammer Miolnir. Slays Jormungander at Ragnarok.

Thrud Thor's daughter.

Thrudheim Thor's realm. Also called Thrudvang.

Titiana Queen of the fairies.

Tyr Son of Frigga and the god of war (with Thor). Eventually kills Garm at Ragnarok.

Uller God of winter, whom Skadi eventually marries.

Urd One of the Norns.

Utgard-loki King of the giants. Tricked Thor.

Vala Another name for Norns.

Valfreya Another name for Freyia.

Valhalla Odin's hall for the celebrated dead warriors chosen by the Valkyrs.

Valkyrs Odin's attendants, led by Freyia. Chose dead warriors to live at Valhalla.

Vanaheim Home of the Vanir.

Vanir Race of gods in conflict with the Aesir; they are gods of the sea and wind.

Vernandi One of the Norns.

Vidar Slays Fenris.

Vigrid The plain where the final battle is held.

Volsung Family of great warriors about whom a great saga was spun.

Wyrd One of the Norns.

Yggdrasill The World Ash, holding up the nine worlds. Does not fall at Ragnarok.

Ymir Giant created from fire and ice; his body created the world.

Further Reading

Clover, C. J., and J. Lindow, *Old Norse-Icelandic Literature: A Critical Guide* (Cornell, 1985)
• Davidson, H. R. E., *Gods and Myths of Northern Europe* (London, 1964) • Hollander, L. M.,
Heimskringla: History of the Kings of Norway (Texas, 1964) • Jones, Gwyn, *A History of the
Vikings* (Oxford, 1984) • Page, R. I., *Norse Myths* (London, 1994) • *The Prose Edda*, translated by
J. I. Young (California, 1966) • Taylor, P. B., *Norse Poems* (London, 1981) • Turville-Petre, E. O. G.,
Myth and Religion in the North (London, 1964)

Notes on Illustrations

Page 3 *Die Walkure*, by Arthur Rackham. Courtesy of Mary Evans Picture Library. **Page 5** *Viking Ships*, by J. H. Valda. Courtesy of
Mary Evans Picture Library. **Page 6** *Das Rhingold* scene 2 – Fasolt & Fafner Kidnap Freyia, by Arthur Rackham. Courtesy of Mary Evans
Picture Library. **Page 9** *The Danes Descend upon the Coast and Possess Northumberland* (Wallington Hall, Northumberland). Courtesy
of the Bridgeman Art Library. **Page 11** *Looking North up McMurdo Strait, Midday, 26th July 1902*, by Edward Adrian Wilson (Royal
Geographical Society, London). Courtesy of the Bridgeman Art Library. **Page 15** *The Palace of the Queen of the Night*, by Karl Friedrich
Schinkel (German Theatre Museum, Munich). **Page 17** *The First Book of Urizen: Man Floating Upside Down*, by William Blake (Private
Collection). Courtesy of the Bridgeman Art Library. **Page 20** *Fallen Angels Entering Pandemonium*, from *Paradise Lost*, by John Martin
(Tate Gallery, London). Courtesy of the Bridgeman Art Library. **Page 22** *Erebos and Northern Islets, McMurdo Strait, Antartica*, by
E. A. Wilson (Royal Geographical Society, London). Courtesy of the Bridgeman Art Library. **Page 25** *Victory O Lord*, by Sir John Everett
Millais (Manchester City Art Galleries). Courtesy of the Bridgeman Art Library. **Page 26** *Imaginary Landscape*, by Thomas Doughty
(Private Collection). Courtesy of the Bridgeman Art Library. **Page 29** *Der Ring: Die Walkure*: Wotan's Farewell to Brunhilde, by Hermann
Hendrich. Courtesy of Mary Evans Picture Library. **Page 31** *Jupiter and Thetis*, by Jean-Auguste Dominique (Musée Granet,
Aix-en-Provence). Courtesy of the Bridgeman Art Library. **Page 34** *Die Gralsburg – the Castle of the Grail*, by Hans Rudolf Schulze.
Courtesy of Mary Evans Picture Library. **Page 37** *Odin and Brunhilde*, by Ferdinand Lercke. Courtesy of Mary Evans Picture Library.
Page 40 *Rainbow Bridge Connecting Heaven and Earth*, by Hermann Hendrich. Courtesy of Mary Evans Picture Library.
Page 43 *Prospero*, by Henry Fussli (York City Art Gallery). Courtesy of the Bridgeman Art Library. **Page 46** *Macbeth and the Witches*,
by Henry Fussli (National Trust, Petworth House, Sussex). Courtesy of the Bridgeman Art Library. **Page 49** *Macbeth and the Witches*,
by Jean Baptiste Camille (Wallace Collection, London). Courtesy of the Bridgeman Art Library. **Page 51** *Sunset in South Tyrol*, by Charles
Morel (York City Art Gallery). Courtesy of the Bridgeman Art Library. **Page 54** *Psyche Loses Sight of his Love*, by Matthew Ridley
Corbett (Borough of Southwark, London). Courtesy of the Bridgeman Art Library. **Page 57** *The Rheinmadchen*, by Arthur Rackham.
Courtesy of Mary Evans Picture Library. **Page 59** *Die Walkure*, Act 3 – Wotan Departs, by Arthur Rackham. Courtesy of Mary Evans
Picture Library. **Page 61** *Der Ring – Das Rheingold* – Loge and the Dragon/Alberich, by Arthur Rackham. Courtesy of Mary Evans
Picture Library. **Page 65** *The Ravager*, by John Charles Dollman (Trustees of the Royal Watercolour Society, London). Courtesy of the
Bridgeman Art Library. **Page 69** Design for the Stage Set of *Daphnis and Chloe* by Ravel, Act I, by Leon Bakst (Musée Des Arts
Decoratifs, Paris). Courtesy of the Bridgeman Art Library. **Page 71** *Das Rheingold*, Scene 4 – Donner, by Arthur Rackham. Courtesy of
Mary Evans Picture Library. **Page 73** *The Viking Sea Raiders*, by Albert Goodwin (Christopher Wood Gallery, London). Courtesy of the
Bridgeman Art Library. **Page 75** *The Giant Polyphemus with Galatea and the Herdsman Acis*, from the Sala di Amore e Psiche, by Giulio
Romano (Palazzo del Te, Mantua). Courtesy of the Bridgeman Art Library. **Page 79** *The Death of Siegfried*, by Hermann Hendrich.
Courtesy of Mary Evans Picture Library. **Page 81** *Neptune Resigning to Briannia the Empire of the Sea*, by William Dyce (Forbes
Magazine Collection, New York). Courtesy of the Bridgeman Art Library. **Page 83** *Siegried*, Act I – *The Wanderer Tells Mime about the
Sword Nothung*, by Arthur Rackham. Courtesy of Mary Evans Picture Library. **Page 85** *The Valkyries*, by Arthur Rackham. Courtesy
of the Mary Evans Picture Library. **Page 89** *The Wooing of Brunhilde*, from *Siegfried and the Twilight of the Gods* by Wagner, by Arthur
Rackham (Private Collection). Courtesy of the Bridgeman Art Library. **Page 90** *Sala dei Giganti*, detail of the *Destruction of the Giants
by Jupiter's Thunderbolts*, by Giulio Romano (Palazzo del Te, Mantua). Courtesy of the Bridgeman Art Library. **Page 93** *Freia, Goddess
of Youth*, by Arthur Rackham. Courtesy of Mary Evans Picture Library. **Page 95** *The Ride of the Valkyrs*, by Hermann Hendrick.
Courtesy of Mary Evans Picture Library. **Page 96** *The Ride of the Valkyries*, by Engel Karl. Courtesy of Christie's Images.
Page 99 *An Iceberg of Cape Evans*, by Edward Adrian Wilson (Cheltenham Art Gallery & Museums, Gloucestershire). Courtesy of the
Bridgeman Art Library. **Page 101** *Viking Ship off Heligland*, by Oscar Schindler. Courtesy of Mary Evans Picture Library.
Page 102 *The Ring, Siegfried Brandishes the Sword Nothung*, by Arthur Rackham. Courtesy of Mary Evans Picture Library.
Page 105 *The Dwarf Laurin*, by Willy Pogany. Courtesy of Mary Evans Picture Library. **Page 106** *The Fairies' Banquet*, by John Anster
Fitzgerald (The Maas Gallery, London). Courtesy of the Bridgeman Art Library. **Page 109** *The Northern Gods Descending*, by William
Collingwood (Bonhams, London). Courtesy of the Bridgeman Art Library. **Page 113** *Neptune Offering Gifts to Venice*, by Giovanni
Battista Tiepolo (Palazzo Ducale, Venice). Courtesy of the Bridgeman Art Library. **Page 117** *Loke Punished*, by J. Doyle Penrose.
Courtesy of the Mary Evans Picture Library. **Page 118** *The Burial of Siegfried*, by Richard Jack (York City Art Gallery). Courtesy of the
Bridgeman Art Library. **Page 121** *The Funeral of a Viking*, Sir Frank Dicksee (Manchester City Art Galleries). Courtesy of the Bridgeman
Art Library. **Page 125** *Siegfried Captures Ludegast*, by Willy Pogany. Courtesy of Mary Evans Picture Libraries.

INDEX